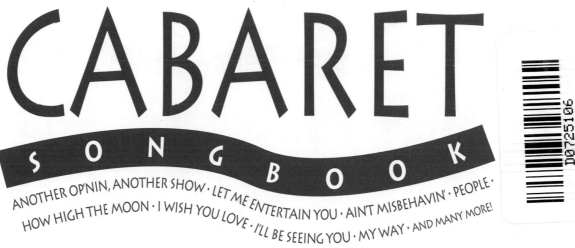

CABARET

SONGBOOK

ANOTHER OP'NIN, ANOTHER SHOW · LET ME ENTERTAIN YOU · AINT MISBEHAVIN' · PEOPLE ·
HOW HIGH THE MOON · I WISH YOU LOVE · I'LL BE SEEING YOU · MY WAY · AND MANY MORE!

HAL•LEONARD®
CORPORATION
7777 W. BLUEMOUND RD. P.O. BOX 13819 MILWAUKEE, WI 53213

Copyright © 1991 by HAL LEONARD PUBLISHING CORPORATION
International Copyright Secured   All Rights Reserved

For all works contained herein:
Unauthorized copying, arranging, adapting, recording or public performance is an infringement of copyright.
Infringers are liable under the law.

ISBN 0-7935-0086-9

COME TO THE CABARET

Cabaret acts should be as carefully crafted as a fine novel with an introduction, the central theme and an ending. You'll want to entertain your audience and play to a wide variety of their emotions. Therefore, your choice of songs and the order in which you present them is critical to your act.

Here are the five basic categories for a twenty to thirty minute act and the areas where you can add additional tunes to intensify or lengthen it.

1 **OPENER**

2 **ESSENCE SONG**
- Adding a third song

3 **BALLAD**
- Adding a second ballad
- Adding a medley of songs
                       or...
- The tour de force song

4 **GRABBER**
- Adding a grabber medley

5 **CLOSER**
- Encores

1 OPENER

This is your introduction and, like any first impression, very important. The song should be an "uptune," i.e., with a lively tempo and a positive lyric — one that will grab the audience's attention. You can give a hint of what's to come via *Comedy Tonight* or letting them know that *Everything's Coming Up Roses*.

An opener is when you "serve the hors d'oeuvres of your set" to whet the audience's appetite for the rest of your act.

2 ESSENCE SONG

Now you can show off a bit more. This song, too, should be an uptune and also should be "you" — the essence of your act. You can be a bit more philosophical, or comedic, or jazzy, and set a tone for the rest of your act as well. You'll be warmed up and the audience settled, so you can really begin to communicate with them.

- **Adding a third song:** Pick one that's slightly down in tempo and intensity from your essence song. Think of it acting as a bridge to your ballad; not a ballad, mind you, but a "bridging device."

3 BALLAD

Here's where your feelings flow, where you sing about love and pluck at heartstrings. The audience will be ready to hear a ballad, to settle down into a dreamy, romantic, or contemplative state.

Since your voice is more exposed during this segment, think carefully about your phrasing and articulation. However, don't be concerned if a ballad isn't your strong point. As long as you project the warmth and feelings of the song, the audience will be with you.

To do something unique when choosing a ballad, you can take an uptune and change the tempo (something that Streisand does well). However, be very sure the lyric works and that you'll have the type of audience that will be open to this change.

- **Adding a second ballad:** This one should come "up" from the first ballad; a "rhythm ballad" as it were. (It could be a jazz or torch song.) Use it as a bridging device into your grabber, or into these next additions...
- **Adding a medley of songs:** This could consist of a certain composer's songs, ethnic songs, a particular artist's songs, songs that talk about the same subject, a series of songs that by their content describe a succession of events (the meeting, the falling in love, the falling out of love, the parting, the reconciliation), etc. This last suggestion is very dramatic, so use it only if you know that you have the kind of audience that loves Wagnerian opera as well.

   or...
- **The tour de force song:** This is the song that will show off your range, your emotions, and your interpretive ability.

4 GRABBER

Okay, now let go and get that audience wild. This is the hand clapping, finger snapping or bodies swaying in their seats part of your performance. (Do watch out for the singalong approach, however. This can really backfire on you if you say, "everybody sing," and they infer by their dead silence, "not me.") Pick a happy, very uptempo song with a message that applies to many people.

- **Adding a grabber medley:** For best audience reactions, this should be no longer than 3½ minutes. Try putting together three songs that successively increase in tempo. Use portions of songs, none in their entirety, and look for smooth segues.

5 CLOSER

Your finale! You've entertained and given your audience a whole gamut of musical experiences and emotions. The *closer* is the ribbon that wraps up and ties up your whole set as a very personal gift. The song should reflect you and the tone of your act and your audience will love it!

- **Encores!** If the audience is clamoring for them, and management and time permit (this is very important), have some choice songs ready. One is usually enough.

PLAYING TO THE HOUSE

You may have heard the phrase "playing to the house" — a very strong consideration when choosing the songs for your act. For instance, you may be in a venue that has a very sophisticated audience (lucky for you). These people will know most any song you sing, and they'll expect to hear some of the more esoteric show songs or those that other cabaret singers have used as signature songs. Or, you might get a group of rowdy conventioneers who require more grabbers and comedy songs to keep their attention. However, if it's prom time, your act may be the "capper" to a special evening out and you may wish to sing more contemporary pop or show songs.

Whatever the venue and audience, be flexible. Be prepared to shuffle your act around and change tunes in order to *play to the house* (be sure your accompanist or back-up group is prepared as well). Of course, if you have a long engagement in one venue, you'll also want to vary your act for repeat customers. However, don't vary your tour de force songs too much, since these tunes are the most memorable and may be one of the reasons you're getting returning fans. It's challenging and exciting to be flexible!

ANOTHER OP'NIN', ANOTHER SHOW
(From "KISS ME, KATE")

Words and Music by COLE PORTER

An - oth - er Op' - nin', An - oth - er Show ___ In Phil - ly, Bos - ton or Balt - i - mo'e, ___ A chance for stage-

- folks to say "Hel - lo" ___ An - oth - er op' - nin' of

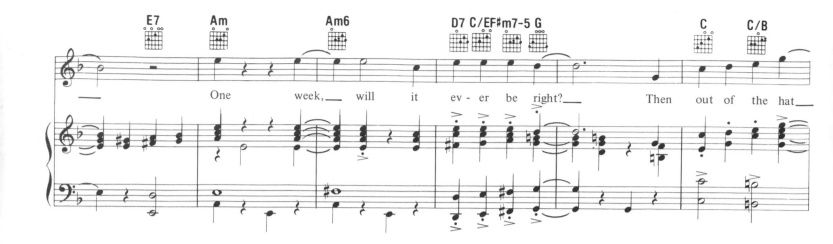

One week,___ will it ev-er be right?___ Then out of the hat___

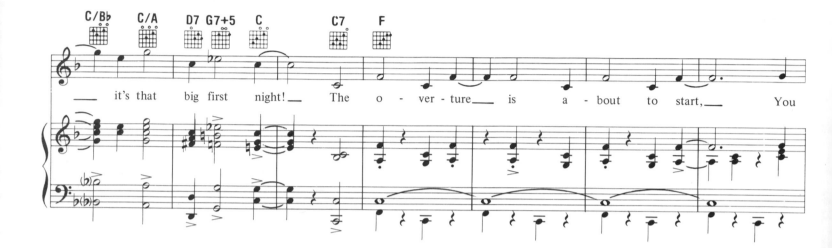

___ it's that big first night!___ The o-ver-ture___ is a-bout to start,___ You

cross your fin-gers and hold your heart,___ It's cur-tain time___ and a-

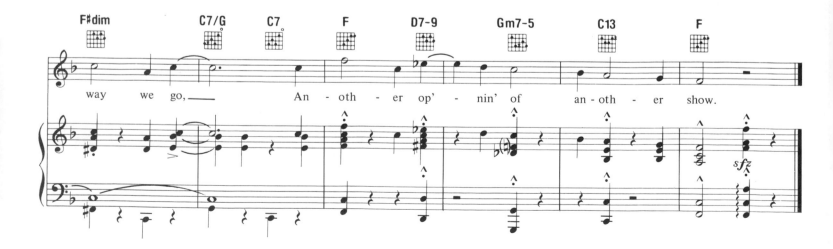

way we go,___ An-oth-er op'-nin' of an-oth-er show.

CABARET
(From The Musical "CABARET")

Music by JOHN KANDER
Words by FRED EBB

COMEDY TONIGHT

Words and Music by
STEPHEN SONDHEIM

Brightly

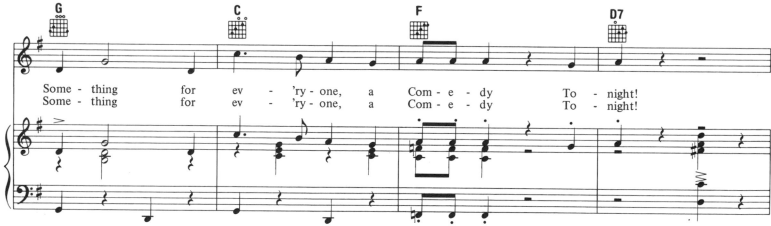

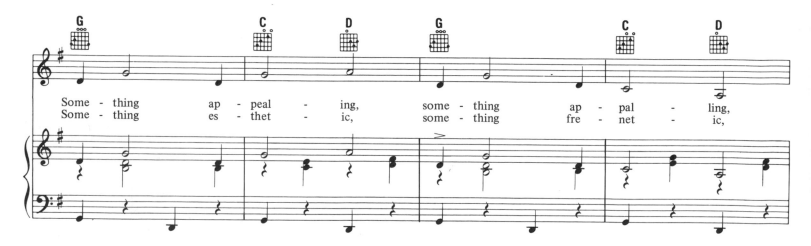

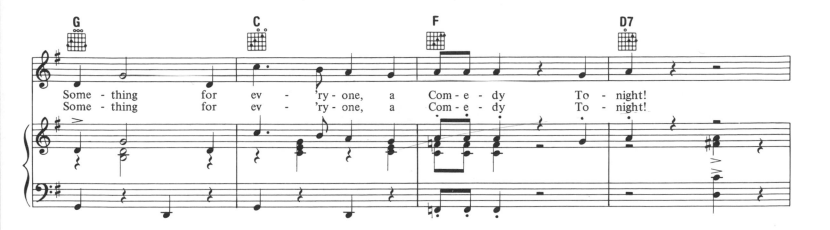

Some - thing for ev - 'ry - one, a Com - e - dy To - night!
Some - thing for ev - 'ry - one, a Com - e - dy To - night!

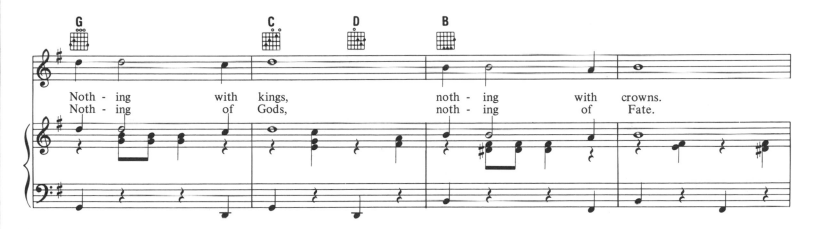

Noth - ing with kings, noth - ing with crowns.
Noth - ing of Gods, noth - ing of Fate.

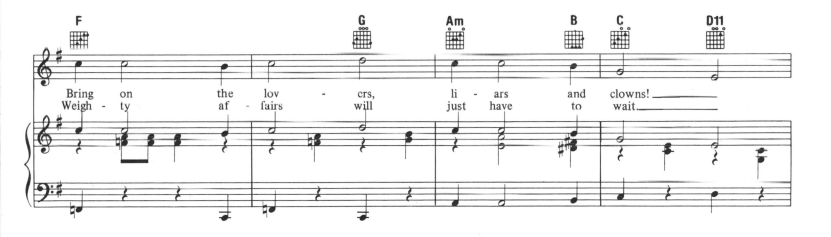

Bring on the lov - ers, li - ars and clowns!_____
Weigh - ty af - fairs will just have to wait._____

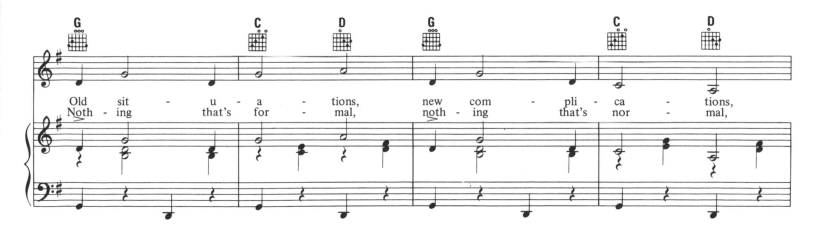

Old sit - u - a - tions, new com - pli - ca - tions,
Noth - ing that's for - mal, noth - ing that's nor - mal,

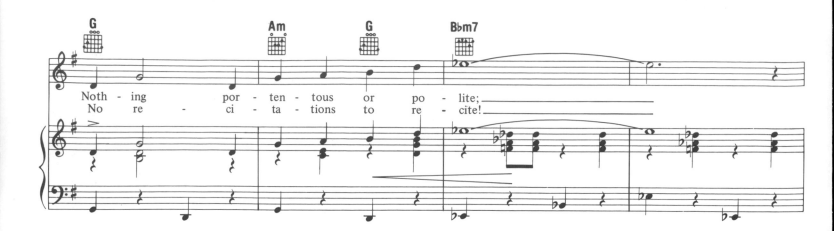

Noth - ing por - ten - tous or po - lite;
No re - ci - ta - tions to re - cite!

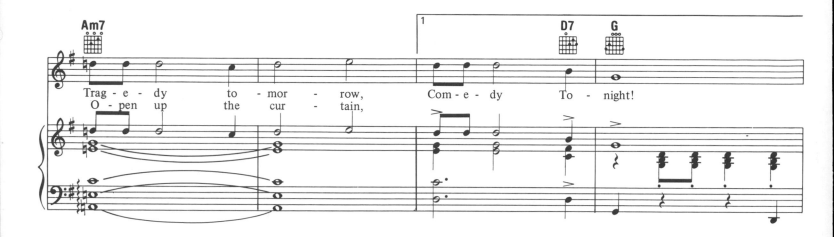

Trag - e - dy to - mor - row,
O - pen up the cur - tain,

Com - e - dy To - night!

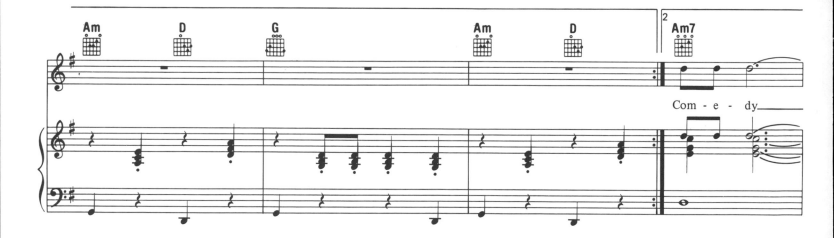

Com - e - dy

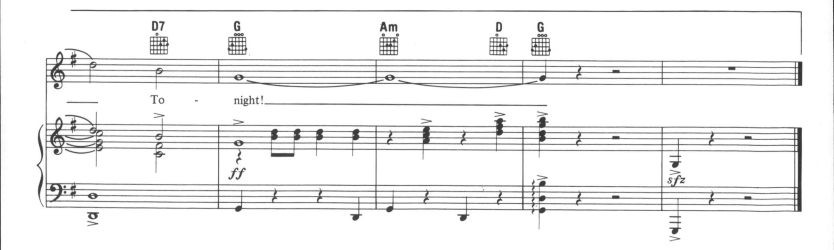

To - night!

EVERYTHING'S COMING UP ROSES

(From "GYPSY")

Words by STEPHEN SONDHEIM
Music by JULE STYNE

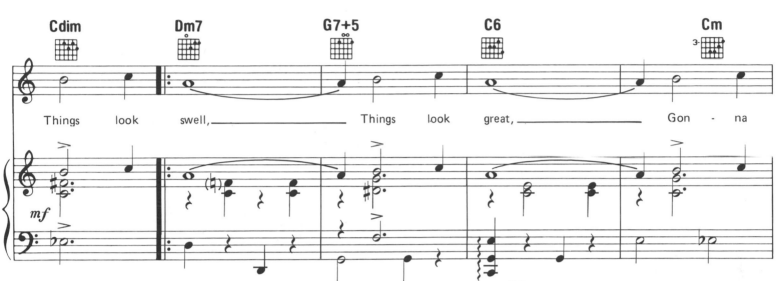

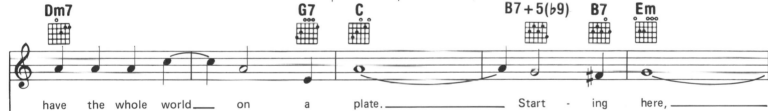

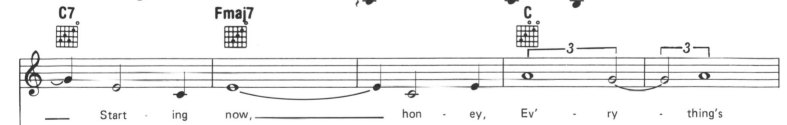

Lyrics:

Things look swell, Things look great, Gon-na have the whole world on a plate. Start-ing here, Start-ing now, hon-ey, Ev'-ry-thing's

19

FROM THIS MOMENT ON

Words and Music by
COLE PORTER

I'VE GOT YOU UNDER MY SKIN

Words and Music by
COLE PORTER

27

LET ME ENTERTAIN YOU

Words by STEPHEN SONDHEIM
Music by JULE STYNE

STARTING HERE, STARTING NOW

Words and Music by
RICHARD MALTBY JR.
and DAVID SHIRE

Quite slowly, with a steady beat

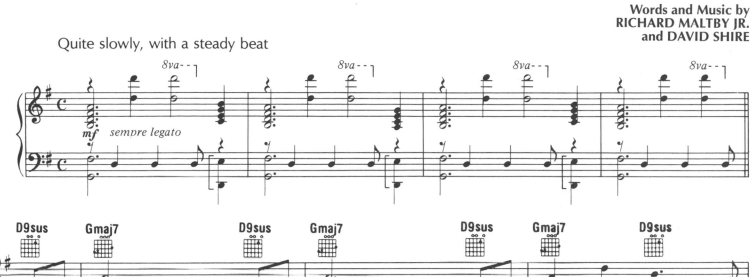

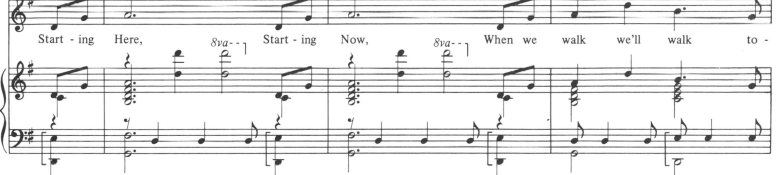

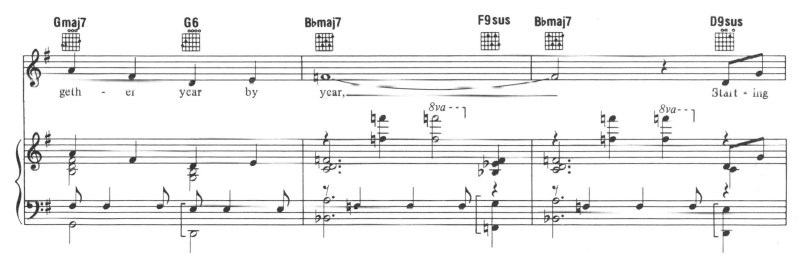

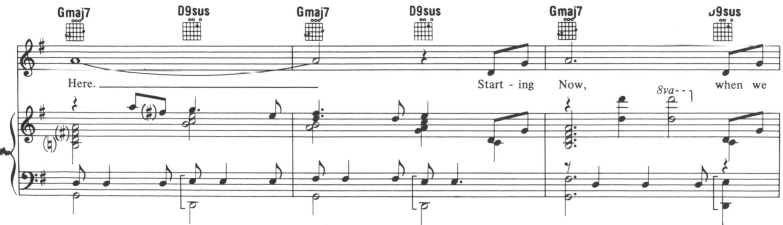

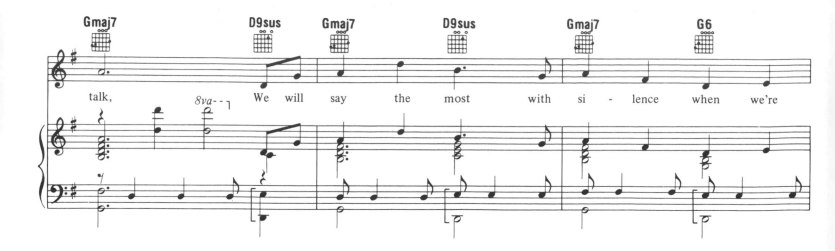

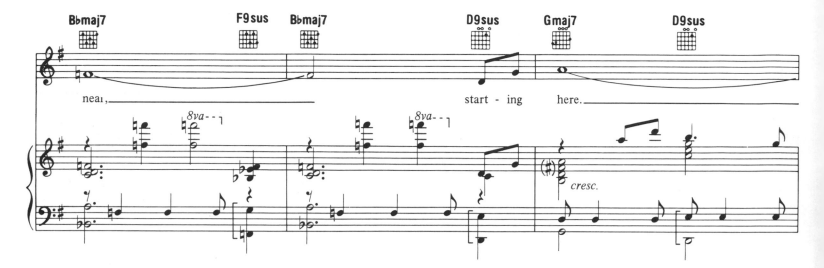

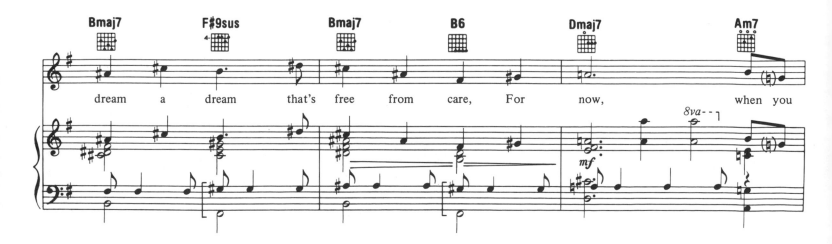

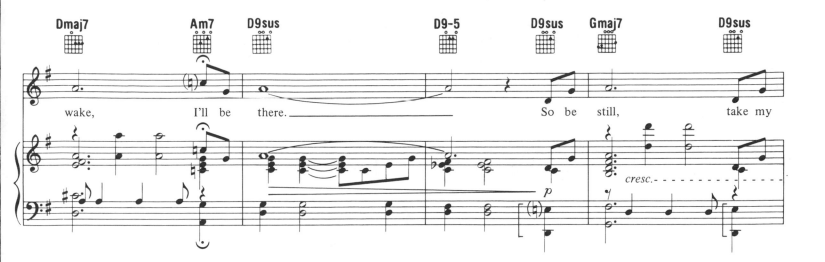

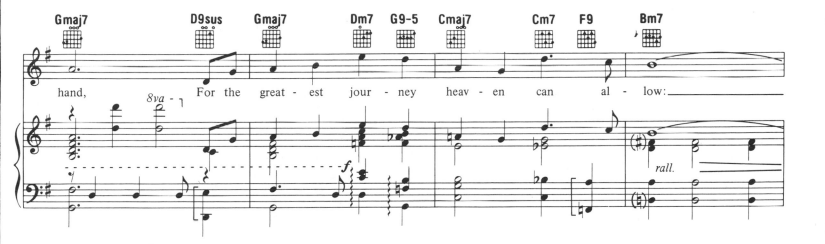

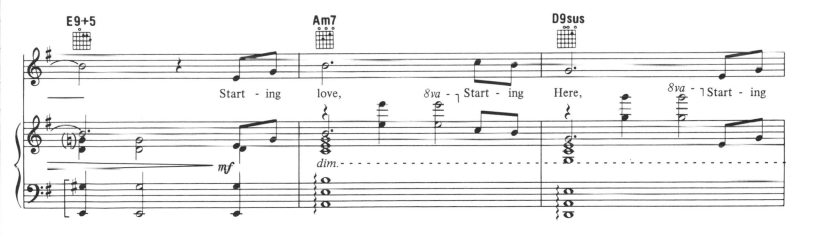

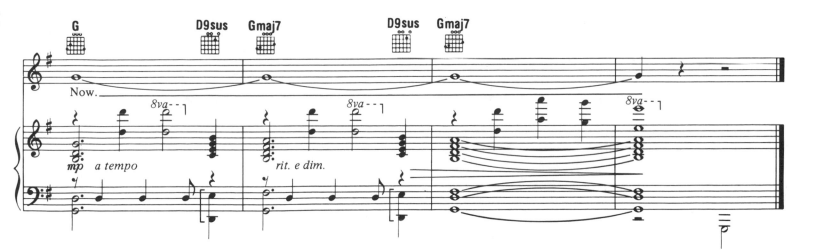

THIS IS MY SONG

(From Charles Chaplin's "A COUNTESS FROM HONG KONG" a Universal Release)

By CHARLES CHAPLIN

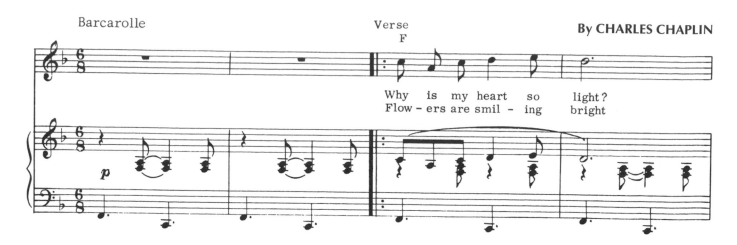

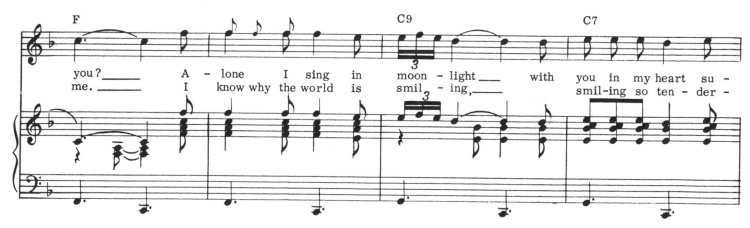

MCA MUSIC PUBLISHING

A WONDERFUL DAY LIKE TODAY

(From the Musical Production
"THE ROAR OF THE GREASEPAINT – THE SMELL OF THE CROWD")

Words & Music by LESLIE BRICUSSE
and ANTHONY NEWLEY

AND ALL THAT JAZZ

Words by FRED EBB
Music by JOHN KANDER

44

THE BEST OF TIMES

(From The Broadway Musical "LA CAGE AUX FOLLES")

Music and Lyric by
JERRY HERMAN

The best of times is now. ___

What's left of sum-mer but a fad-ed rose? ___

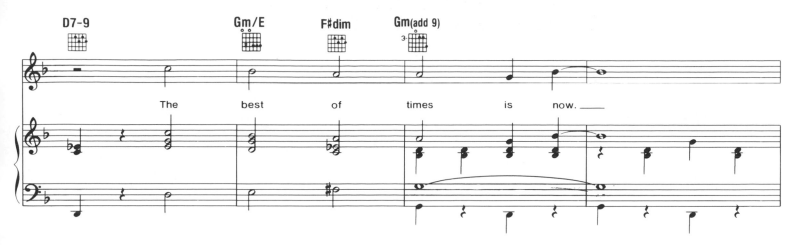

The best of times is now. ___

As for to-mor-row, well, who knows? Who knows? Who

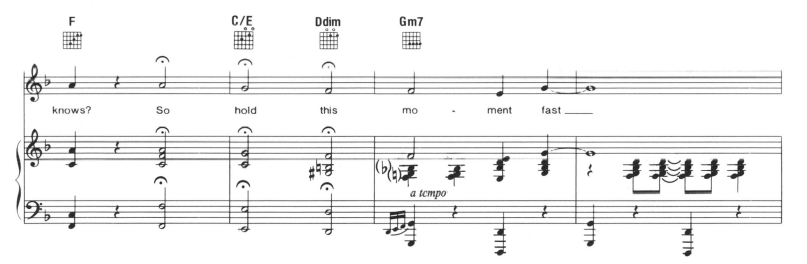

knows? So hold this mo-ment fast ___

and live and love as hard as you know how. ___

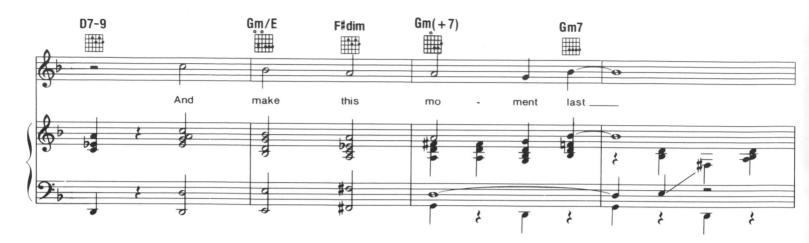

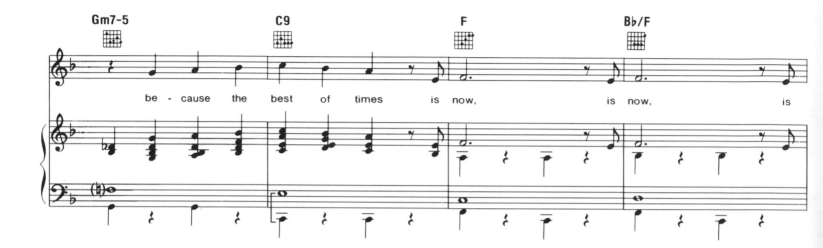

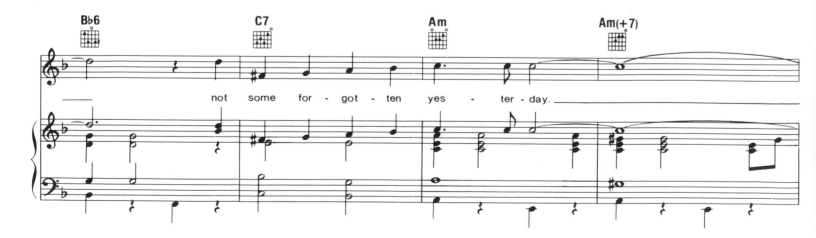

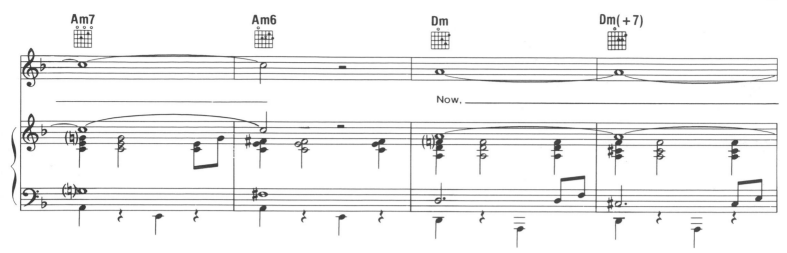

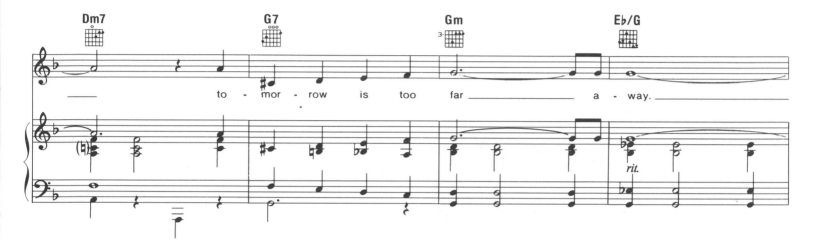

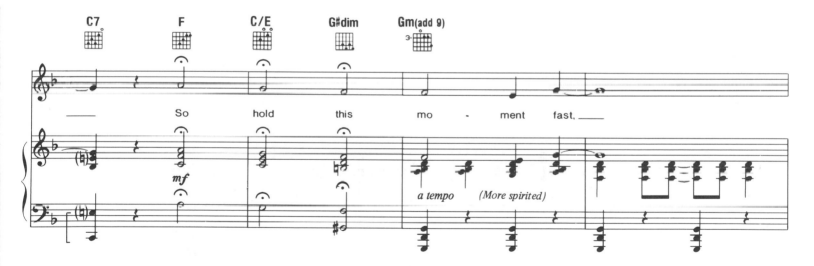

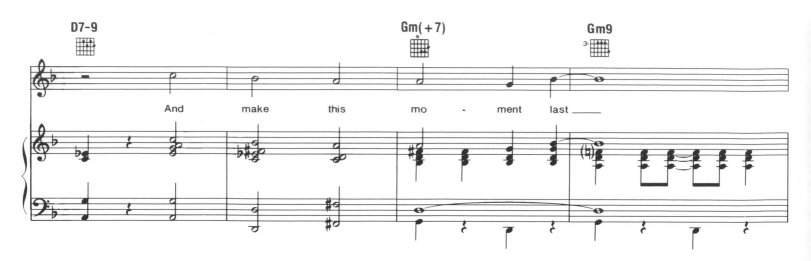

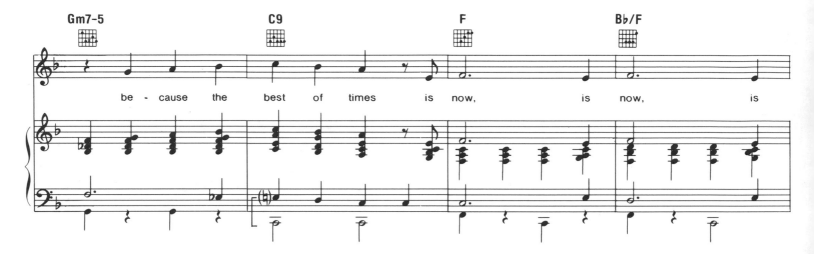

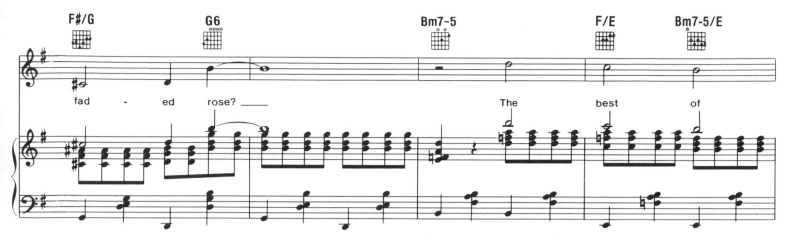

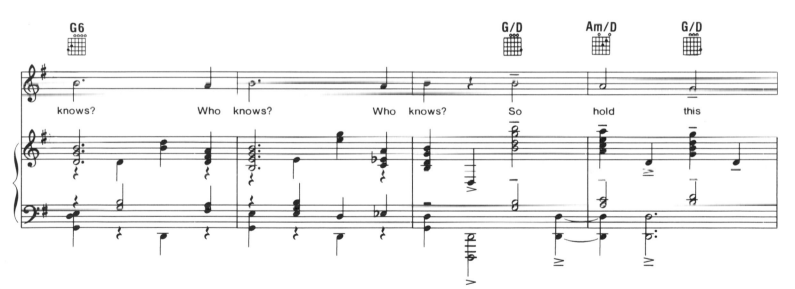

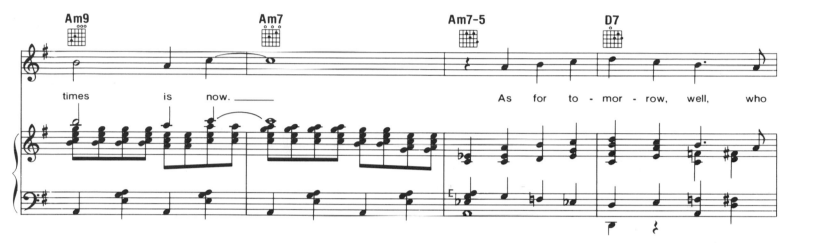

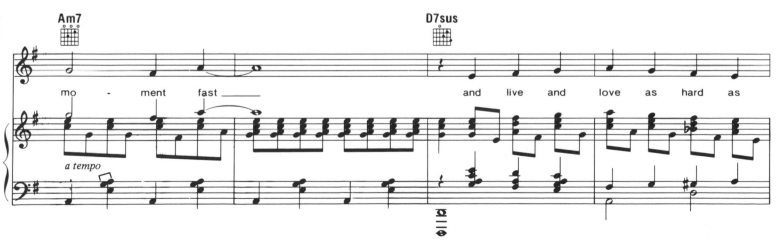

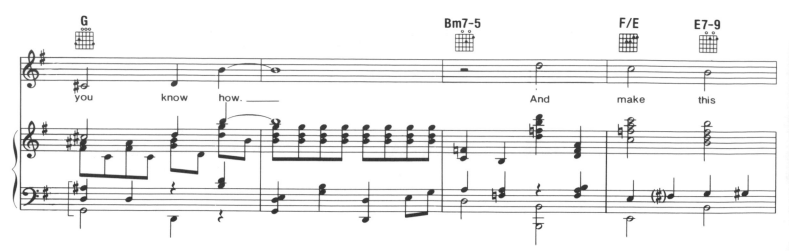

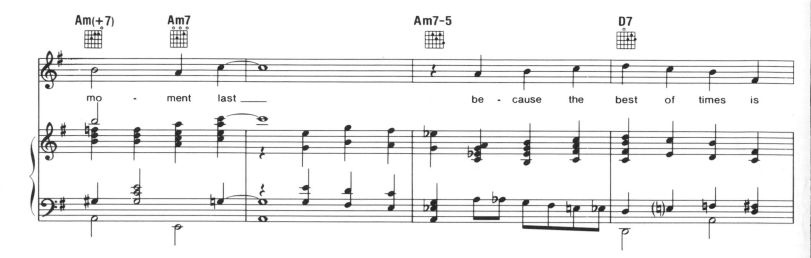

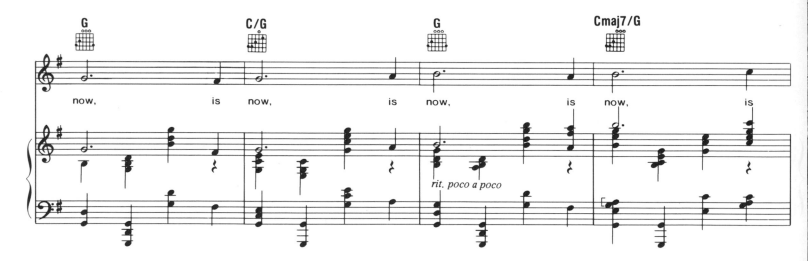

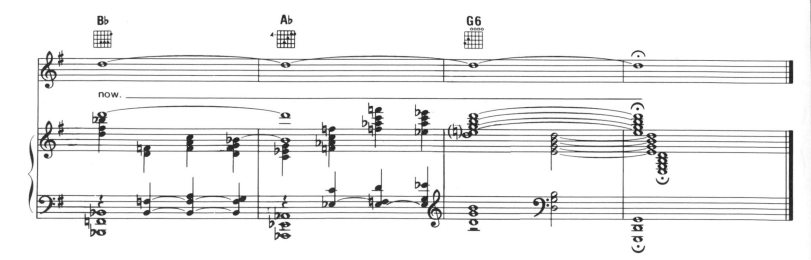

I'VE GOT YOUR NUMBER

Music by CY COLEMAN
Lyric by CAROLYN LEIGH

Moderate, with a relaxed swinging beat

I've Got Your Num-ber,___ I know you in-side___ out,

You ain't no Ea-gle___ Scout, You're all at sea!

Oh, yes, you'll brag a lot,___ Wave your own___ flag a lot,___

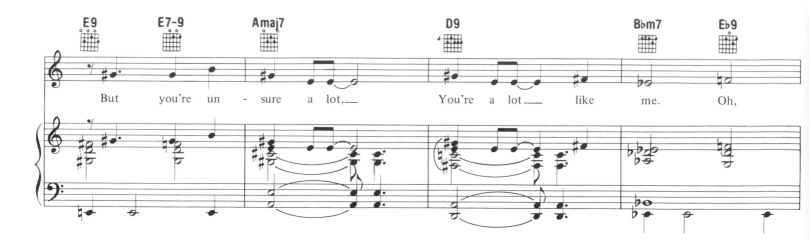

But you're un - sure a lot,___ You're a lot___ like me. Oh,

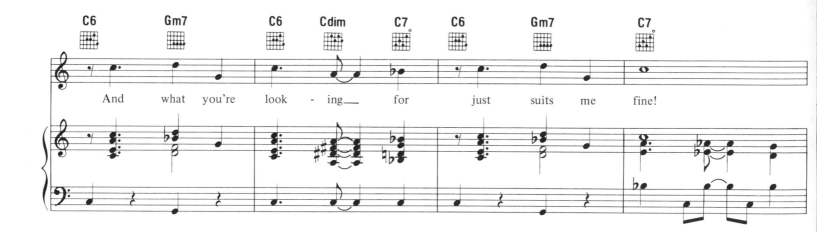

I've Got Your Num - ber___ And what you're look - ing___ for

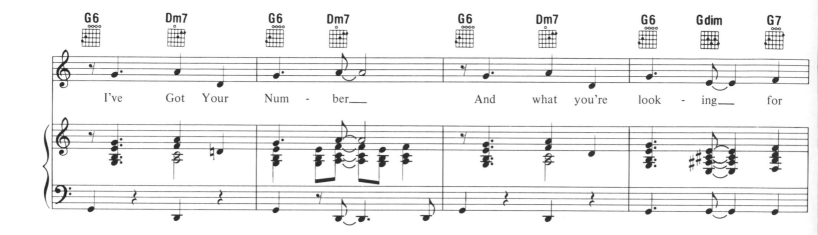

And what you're look - ing___ for just suits me fine!

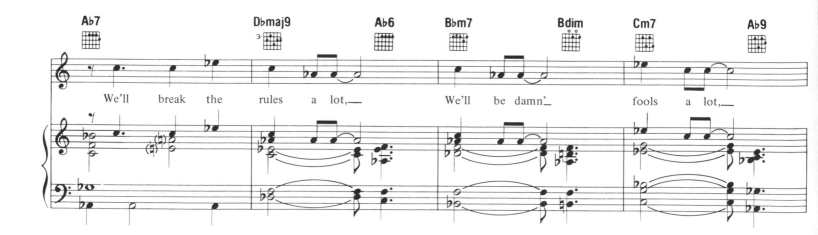

We'll break the rules a lot,___ We'll be damn'___ fools a lot,___

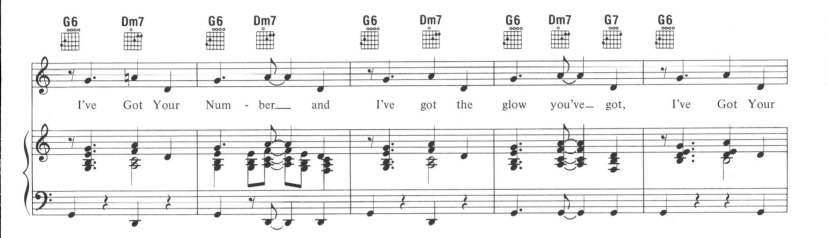

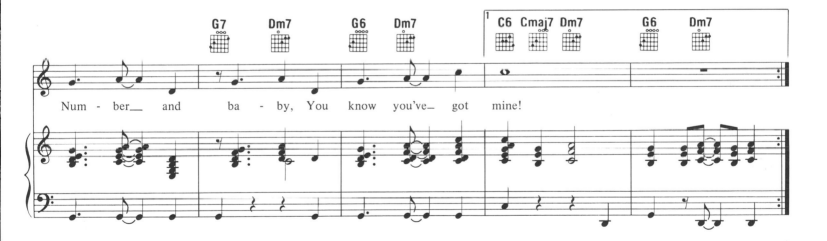

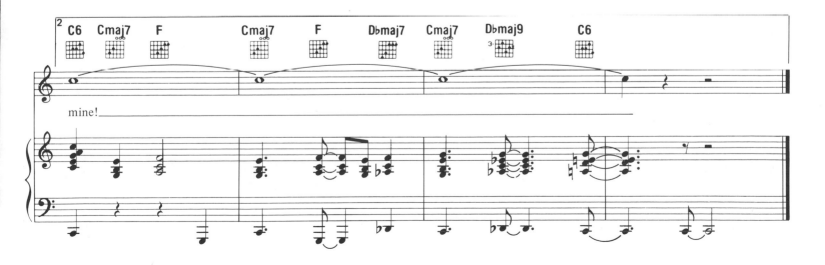

LUCK BE A LADY
(From "GUYS AND DOLLS")

Words and Music by
FRANK LOESSER

They call you La-dy Luck but there is room for doubt At

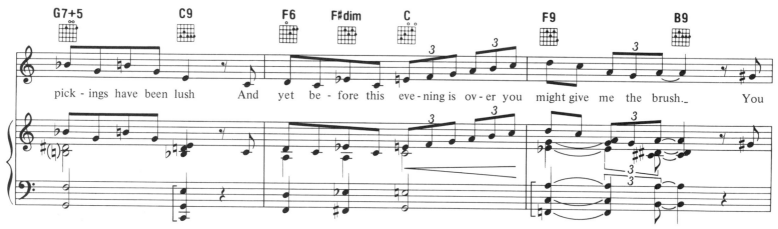

times you have a ver-y un-la-dy like way of run-ning out,_ You're on a date with me the

pick-ings have been lush And yet be-fore this eve-ning is ov-er you might give me the brush._ You

might for-get your man-ners, you might re-fuse to stay, And so the best that I can do is

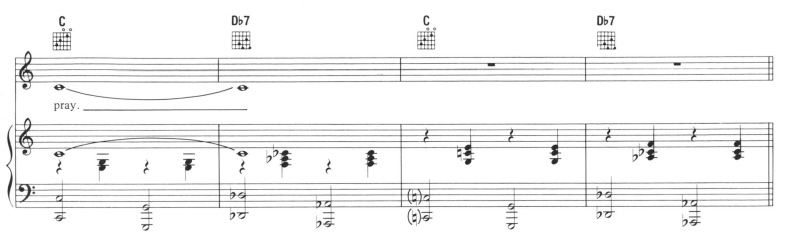

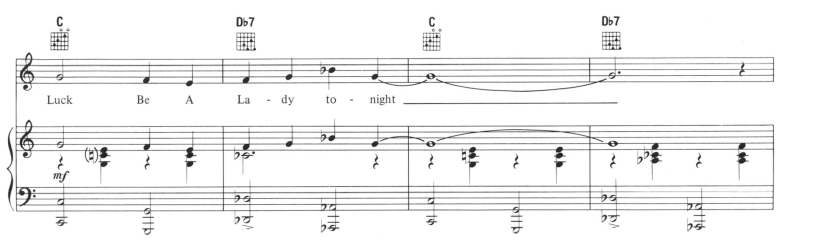

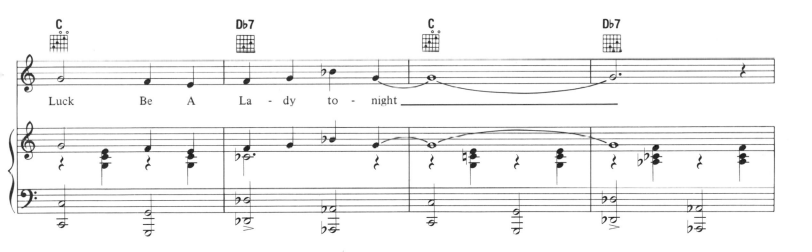

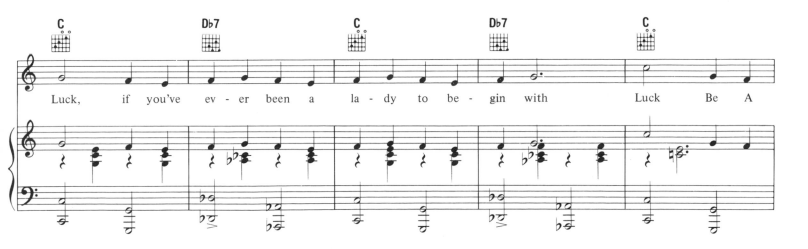

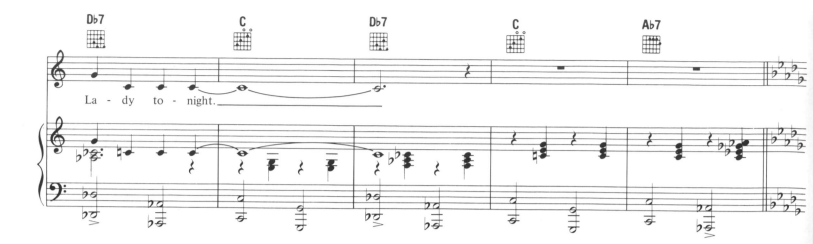

La - dy to - night.

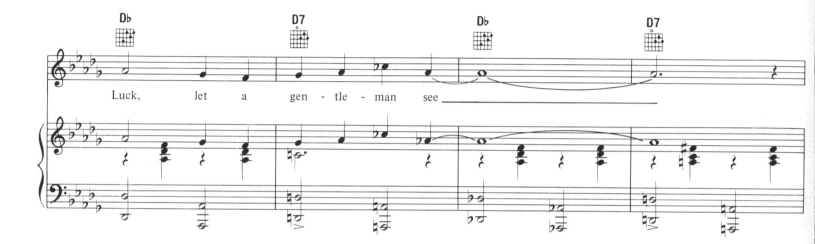

Luck, let a gen - tle - man see _____

How nice a dame you can be _____

I know the way you've treat - ed oth - er guys you've been with Luck Be A

AT LONG LAST LOVE

Words and Music by
COLE PORTER

I'D DO ANYTHING
(From the Columbia Pictures-Romulus film "OLIVER")

Words and Music by
LIONEL BART

ev - 'ry - thing for one kiss ev - 'ry - thing; Yes,
ev - 'ry - thing for one kiss ev - 'ry - thing; Yes,
life and limb To keep you in the swim; Yes,

I'd do an - y - thing, An - y - thing?
I'd do an - y - thing, An - y - thing?
We'd do an - y - thing, An - y - thing?

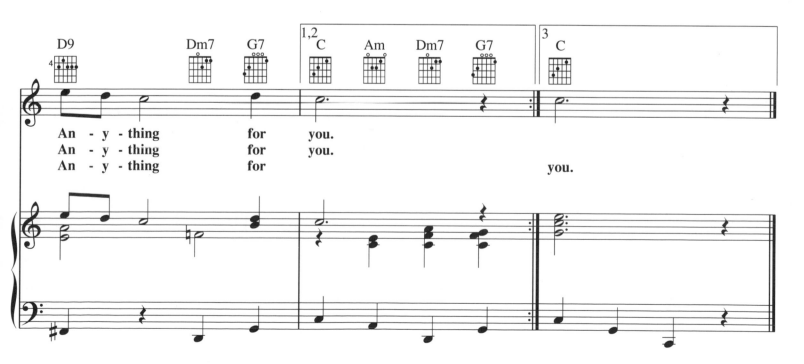

An - y - thing for you.
An - y - thing for you.
An - y - thing for you.

THE JOKER

(From the Musical Production "THE ROAR OF THE GREASEPAINT-The Smell Of The Crowd")

Words and Music by LESLIE BRICUSSE
and ANTHONY NEWLY

72

73

I'M ALWAYS DRUNK
IN SAN FRANCISCO

Words and Music by
TOMMY WOLF

COMES LOVE

Words and Music by LEW BROWN,
SAM H. STEPT & CHARLIE TOBIAS

SING FOR YOUR SUPPER

Moderate and Graceful

Words by LORENZ HART
Music by RICHARD RODGERS

Hawks and crows do lots of things, But the ca-na-ry on-ly sings.

She is a cour-te-san on wings, So I've heard.

Ea-gles and storks are twice as strong, All the ca-na-ry knows is song,

I'M BEGINNING TO SEE THE LIGHT

Words and Music by HARRY JAMES, DUKE ELLINGTON,
JOHNNY HODGES and DON GEORGE

HOW HIGH THE MOON
(From "TWO FOR THE SHOW")

Words by NANCY HAMILTON
Music by MORGAN LEWIS

AIN'T MISBEHAVIN'

Words by ANDY RAZAF
Music by THOMAS WALLER
and HARRY BROOKS

Moderately

No-one to talk with, all by my-self, No one to walk with, but I'm hap-py on___ the shelf.

Ain't Mis-be-hav-in', I'm sav-in' my love for you._____

I know for cer-tain the one I love I'm thru with flirt-in', it's just you I'm think-in' of,

MAYBE THIS TIME

Lyric by FRED EBB
Music by JOHN KANDER

97

BLAME IT ON MY YOUTH

Words by EDWARD HEYMAN
Music by OSCAR LEVANT

Like a child of three, You _____ meant more than

an - y - thing, All the world to me!

If you were on my mind____ all night and day, Blame it on my youth;___

____ If I for - got to eat ____ and sleep and

BY MYSELF

Words by HOWARD DIETZ
Music by ARTHUR SCHWARTZ

DOWN IN THE DEPTHS
(On The Ninetieth Floor)

Words and Music by
COLE PORTER

some-bod-y else, And walks out._____ With a

mil - lion Ne - on rain - bows burn-ing be - low me,_____

And a mil - lion blaz - ing tax - is rais-ing a

roar,_____ Here I sit a - bove the

MAD ABOUT THE BOY

Words and Music by
NOEL COWARD

met him at a par-ty just a cou-ple of years a-go, He was rath-er o-ver heart-y and ri-

dic-u-lous, But as I'd seen him on the screen he cast a cer - tain

I WISH YOU LOVE

English Lyric by ALBERT A. BEACH
French Lyric and Music by CHARLES TRENET

MCA MUSIC PUBLISHING

I'M GLAD THERE IS YOU
(In This World Of Ordinary People)

Words and Music by PAUL MADEIRA
and JIMMY DORSEY

LITTLE GIRL BLUE

Words by LORENZ HART
Music by RICHARD RODGERS

MY FUNNY VALENTINE

(From "BABES IN ARMS")

Words by LORENZ HART
Music by RICHARD RODGERS

MY SHIP
(From The Musical Production "LADY IN THE DARK")

Words by IRA GERSHWIN
Music by KURT WEILL

MY LOVE IS A WANDERER

Words and Music by
BART HOWARD

Lyrics:

My love is a wan-der-er, wan-d'ring o-ver land and sea,_____ And I am a won-der-er, won-d'ring: Does my love, love me?_____ { He } sent a
{ She }

Fmaj7 F6 Gm7 C7♭9 F F6 Gm7 C7
then, from Par - is came a line "Feel - in' fine
F A♭dim Gm7 C7 Dm7♭5
Now, my love, off to Rome!" Noth - ing of com - ing
F/G G7 C G F G7 C Am
home. But in {his her} card this morn - ing {He She} said the
Dm7 G7 Em Am Em7 Fmaj7 F G7♭9 1 C
dear - est thing, "Meet me in Shan - non in the spring!"

SHE (HE) TOUCHED ME

Lyric by IRA LEVIN
Music by MILTON SCHAFER

Gracefully

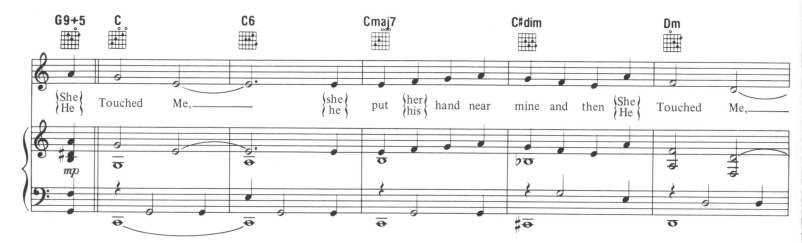

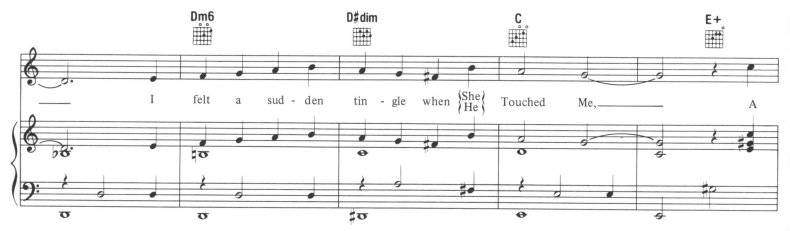

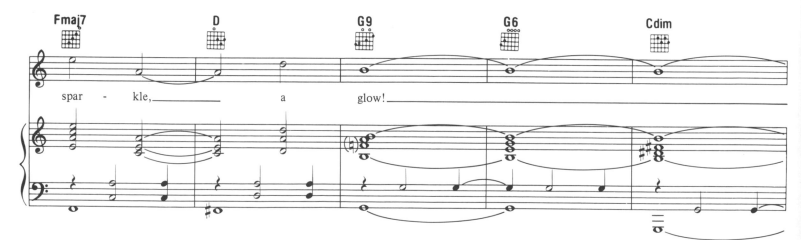

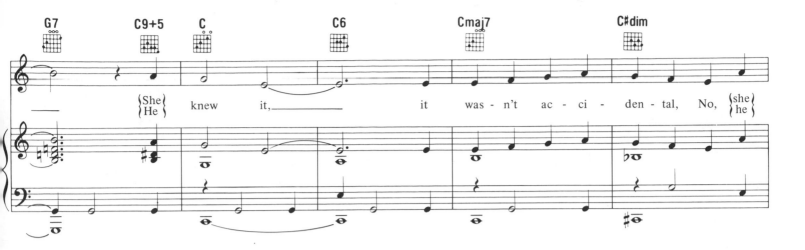

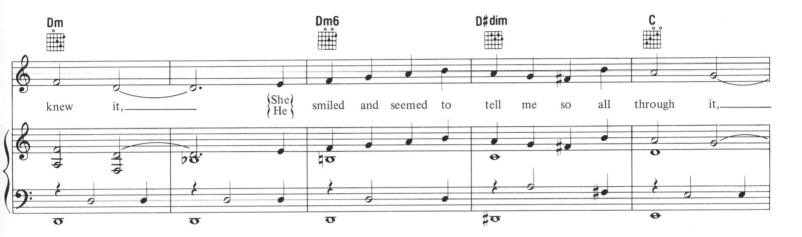

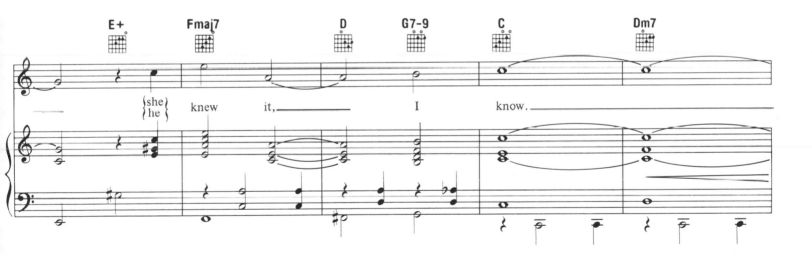

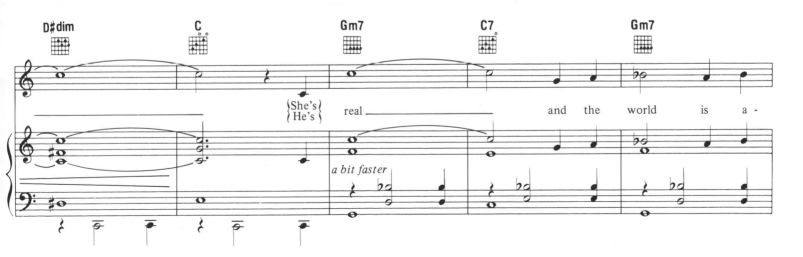

live and shin - ing, _____ I

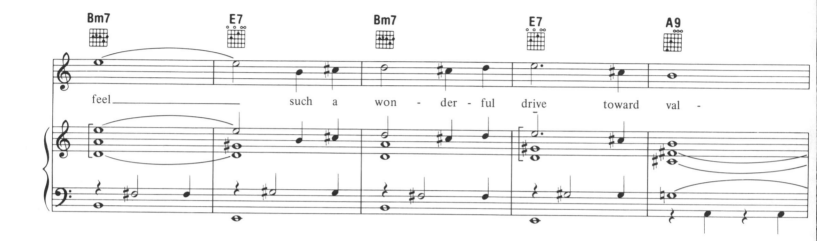

feel _____ such a won - der - ful drive toward val -

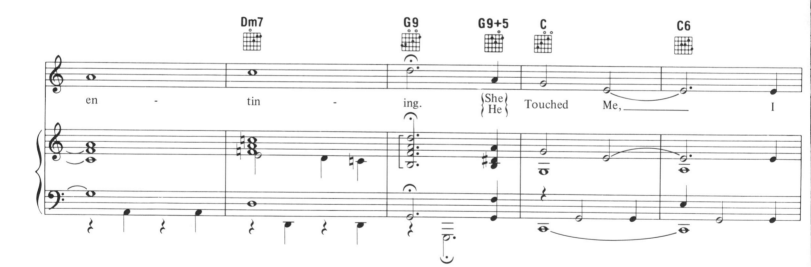

en - tin - ing. {She}{He} Touched Me, _____ I

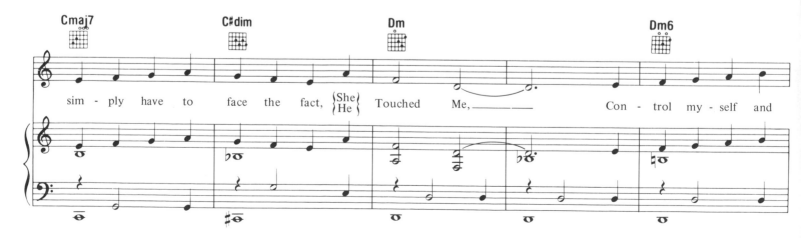

sim - ply have to face the fact, {She}{He} Touched Me, _____ Con - trol my - self and

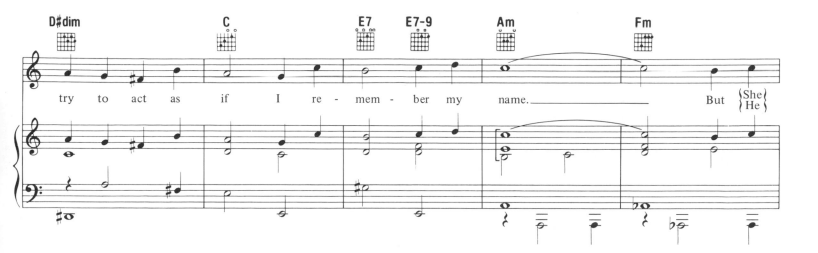

try to act as if I re-mem-ber my name._____ But {She}{He}

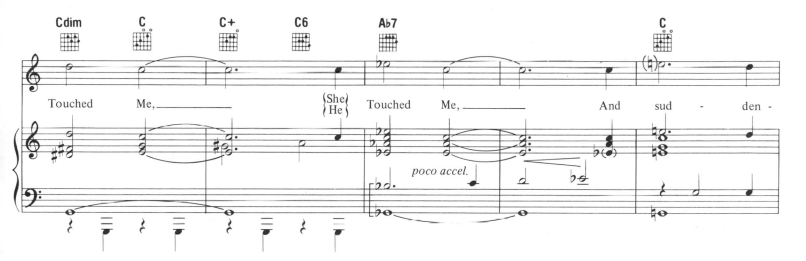

Touched Me,_____ {She}{He} Touched Me,_____ And sud-den-

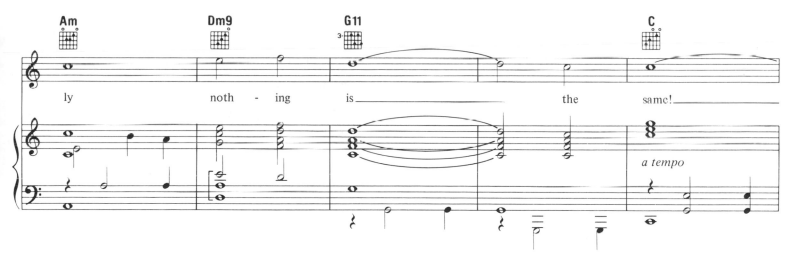

ly noth-ing is_____ the same!_____

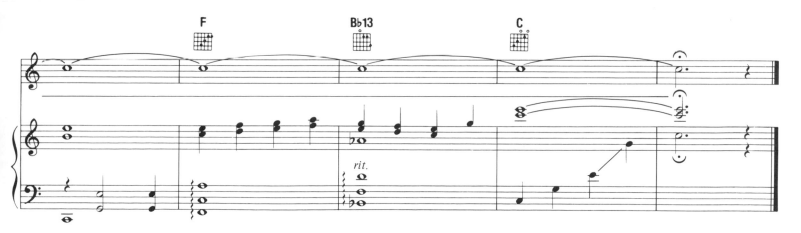

AC-CENT-TCHU-ATE
THE POSITIVE

Lyrics by JOHNNY MERCER
Music by HAROLD ARLEN

Moderately (with a steady rock)

ANY PLACE I HANG MY HAT IS HOME

Words by JOHNNY MERCER
Music by HAROLD ARLEN

152

BEING ALIVE
(From "COMPANY")

Words and Music by
STEPHEN SONDHEIM

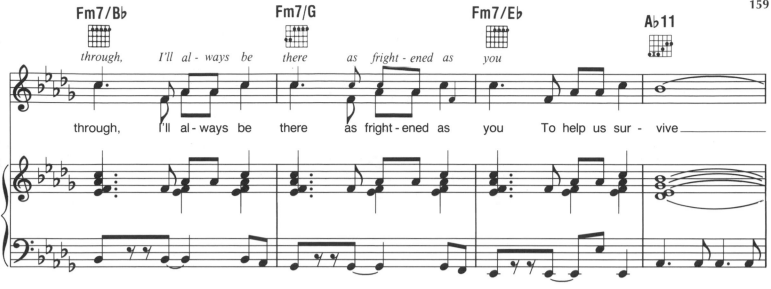

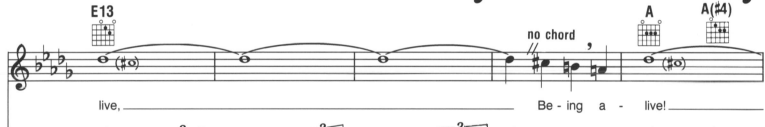

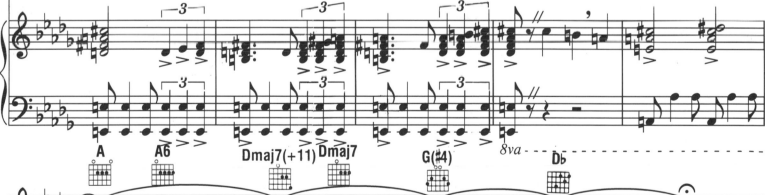

THE BEST IS YET TO COME

Lyrics by CAROLYN LEIGH
Music by CY COLEMAN

Moderately, with a beat

Out of the tree of life___ I just picked me a plum,___

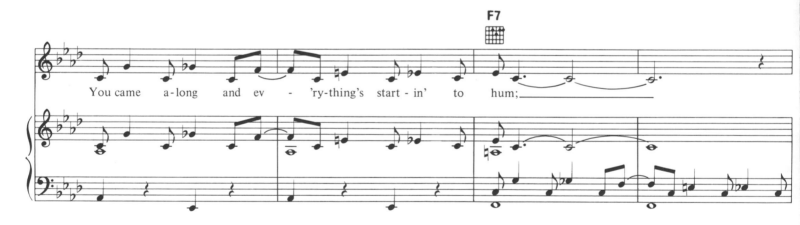

You came a-long and ev-'ry-thing's start-in' to hum;___

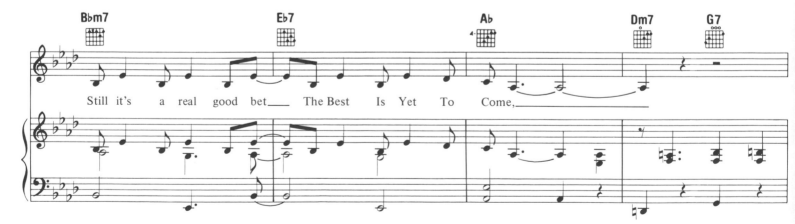

Still it's a real good bet___ The Best Is Yet To Come,___

The Best Is Yet To Come and babe, won't it be fine,_____

You think you've seen the sun___ but you ain't seen it shine,_____

Wait till the warm-up's un-der way,___ Wait till our lips have met,___

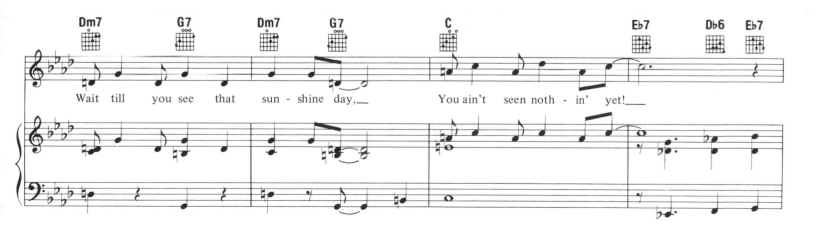

Wait till you see that sun-shine day,___ You ain't seen noth-in' yet!___

The Best Is Yet To Come and babe, won't it be fine,

The Best Is Yet To Come, come the day you're mine.

mine. Come the day you're mine, I'm gon-na teach you to

fly; We've on-ly tast-ed the wine, We're gon-na drain the cup

dry. Wait till your charms are ripe for these arms to sur-round,

COPACABANA
(At The Copa)

Words by BRUCE SUSSMAN
and JACK FELDMAN
Music by BARRY MANILOW

Moderately, with a Latin 'feel'

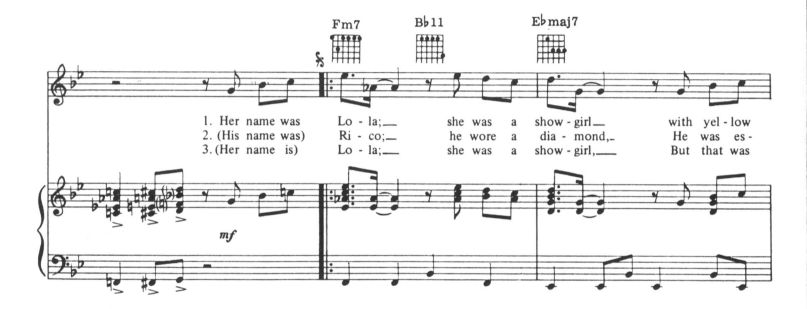

1. Her name was Lo - la;__ she was a show - girl__ with yel - low
2. (His name was) Ri - co;__ he wore a dia - mond,__ He was es -
3. (Her name is) Lo - la;__ she was a show - girl,__ But that was

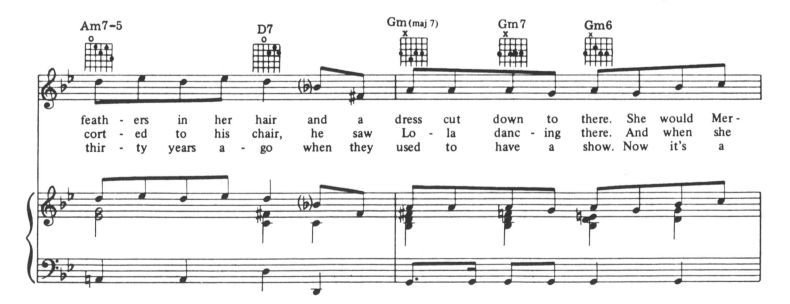

feath - ers in her hair and a dress cut down to there. She would Mer -
cort - ed to his chair, he saw Lo - la danc - ing there. And when she
thir - ty years a - go when they used to have a show. Now it's a

166

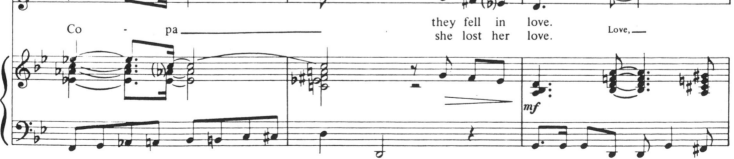

167

I BELIEVE IN YOU
(From "HOW TO SUCCEED IN BUSINESS WITHOUT REALLY TRYING")

Words and Music by
FRANK LOESSER

172

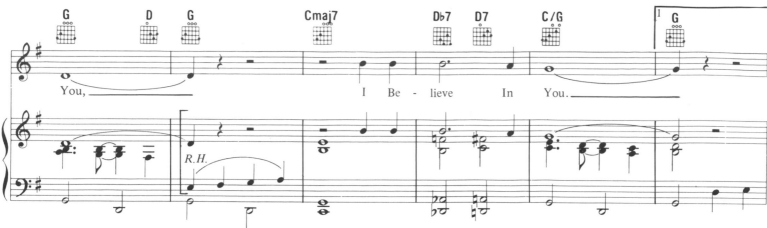

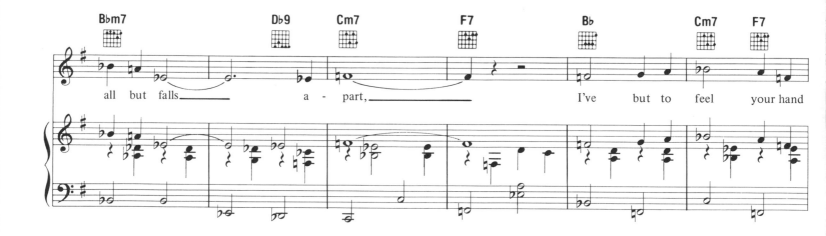

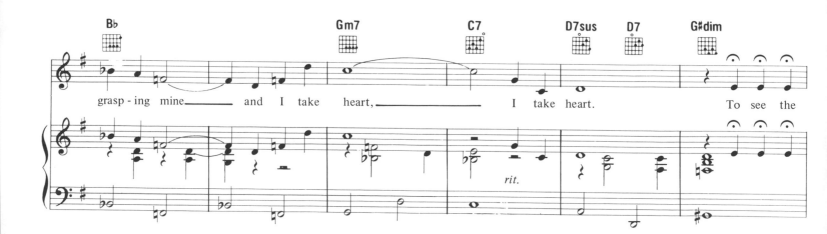

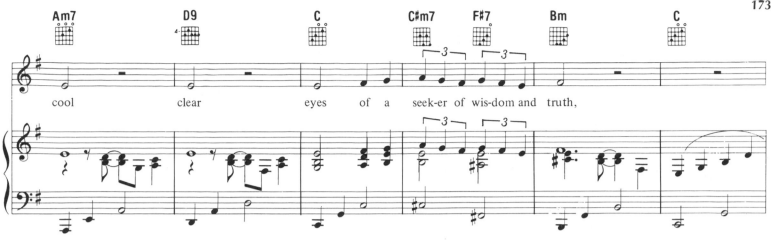

cool   clear   eyes   of   a   seek-er of wis-dom and   truth,

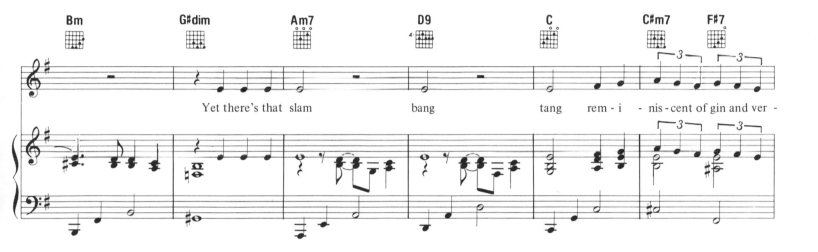

Yet there's that slam   bang   tang   rem - i - nis-cent of gin and ver -

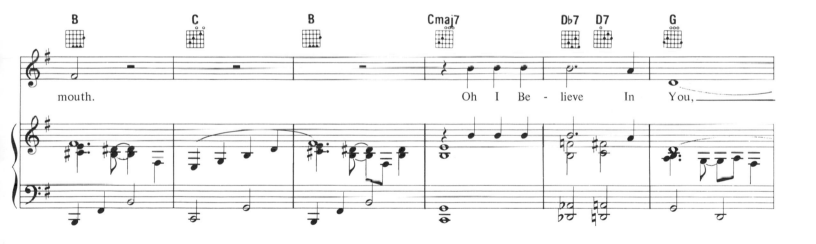

mouth.   Oh I Be - lieve In You, ____

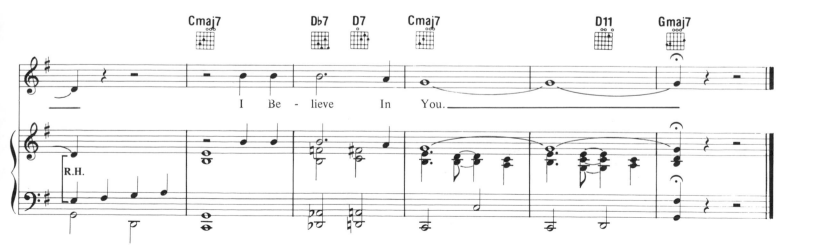

I Be - lieve In You. ____

IT'S ALL RIGHT WITH ME

Words and Music by
COLE PORTER

Steadily moving fox trot

It's the wrong time _____ and the wrong place _____ tho' your face is charm-

-ing it's the wrong face, _____ it's not {her}{his} face _____ but such a charm-ing face _____

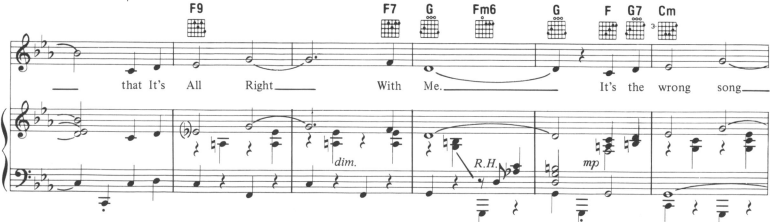

that It's All Right _____ With Me. _____ It's the wrong song _____

PIANO MAN

Words and Music by
BILLY JOEL

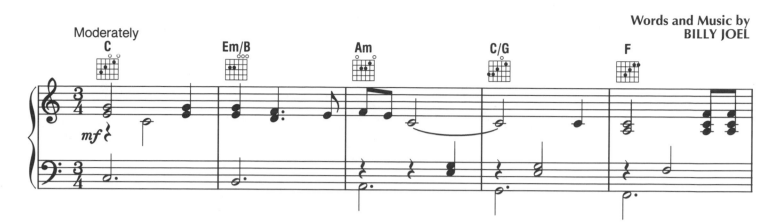

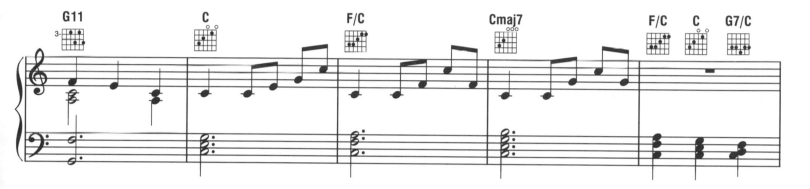

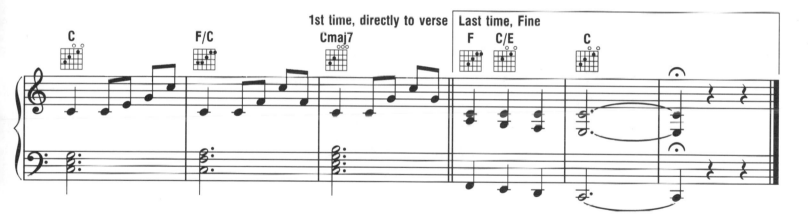

1st time, directly to verse Last time, Fine

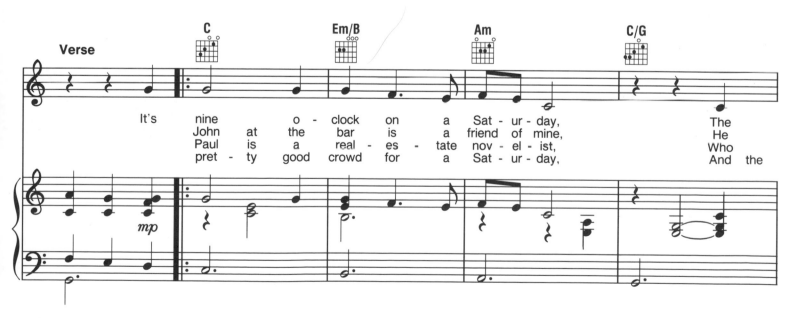

Verse

It's nine o - clock on a Sat - ur - day,   The
John at the bar is a friend of mine,   He
Paul is a real - es - tate nov - el - ist,   Who
pret - ty good crowd for a Sat - ur - day,   And the

reg - u - lar crowd shuf - fles ___ in ___ There's an
gets me my drinks for ___ free, ___ And he's
nev - er had time for a ___ wife ___ And he's
man - ag - er gives me a ___ smile ___ 'Cause he

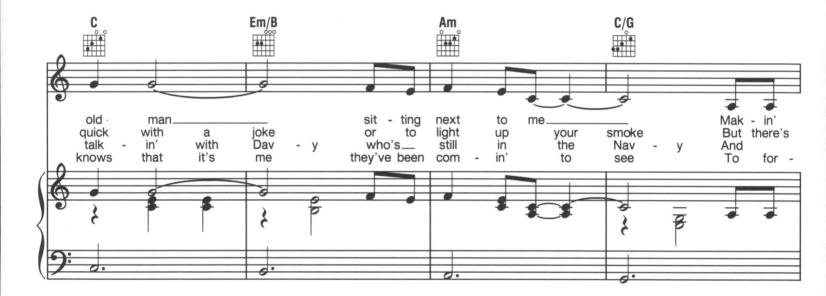

old · man ___ sit - ting next to me ___ Mak - in'
quick with a joke or to light up your smoke But there's
talk - in' with Dav - y who's_ still in the Nav - y And
knows that it's me they've been com - in' to see To for -

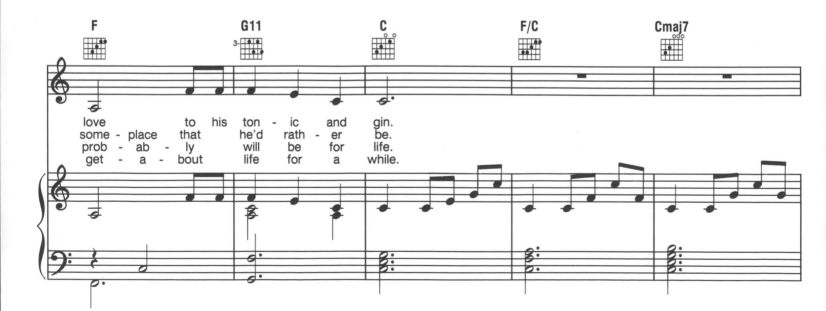

love to his ton - ic and gin.
some - place that he'd rath - er be.
prob - ab - ly will be for life.
get - a - bout life for a while.

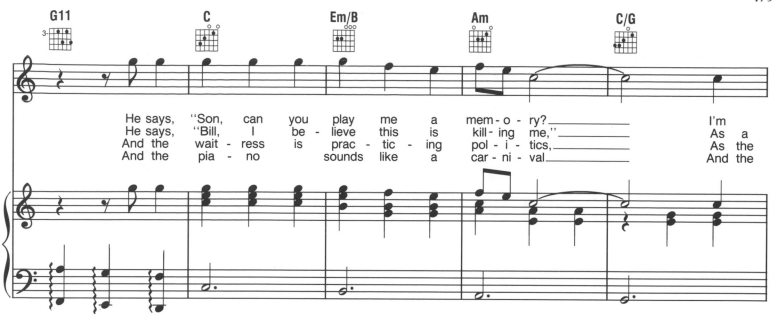

He says, "Son, can you play me a mem - o - ry?_____ I'm
He says, "Bill, I be - lieve this is kill - ing me,"_____ As a
And the wait - ress is prac - tic - ing pol - i - tics,_____ As the
And the pia - no sounds like a car - ni - val_____ And the

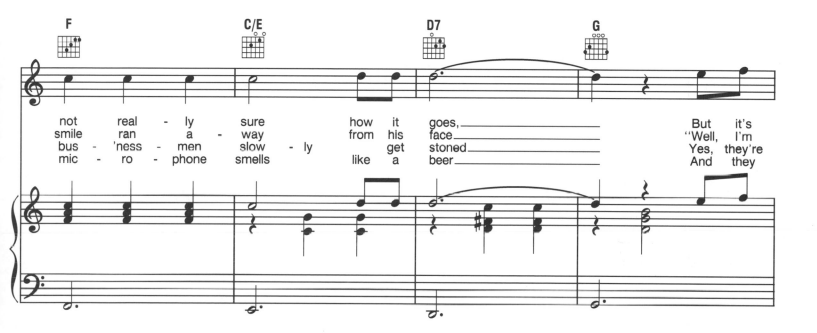

not real - ly sure how it goes,_____ But it's
smile ran a - way from his face_____ "Well, I'm
bus - 'ness - men slow - ly get stoned_____ Yes, they're
mic - ro - phone smells like a beer_____ And they

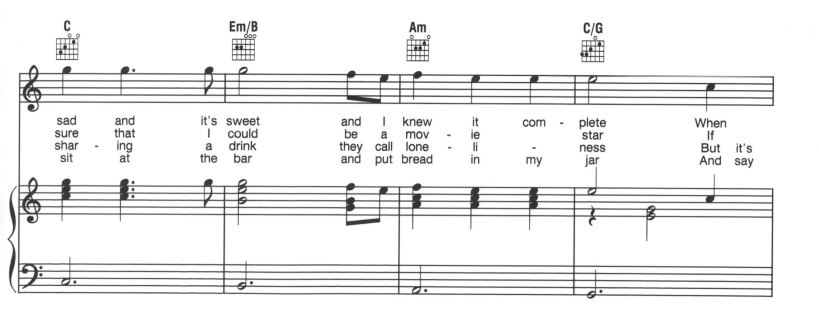

sad and it's sweet and I knew it com - plete When
sure that I could be a mov - ie star If
shar - ing a drink they call lone - li - ness But it's
sit at the bar and put bread in my jar And say

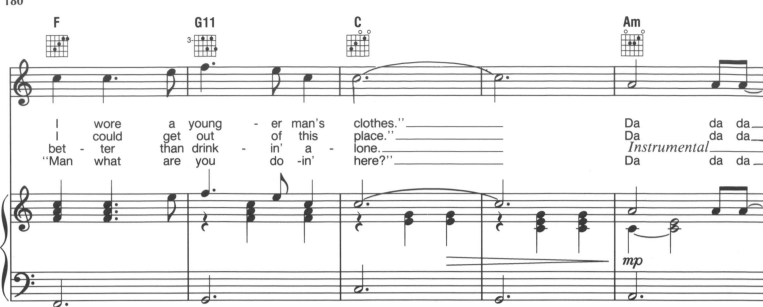

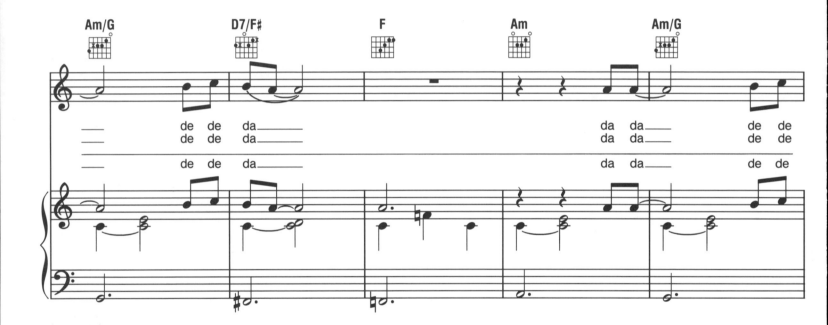

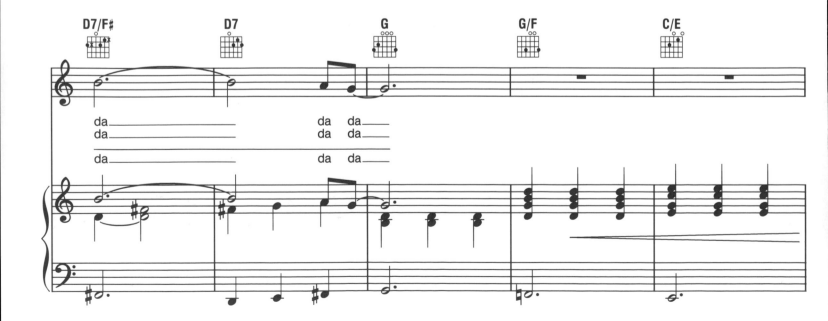

THERE WILL NEVER BE ANOTHER YOU

Lyric by MACK GORDON
Music by HARRY WARREN

Sweetly

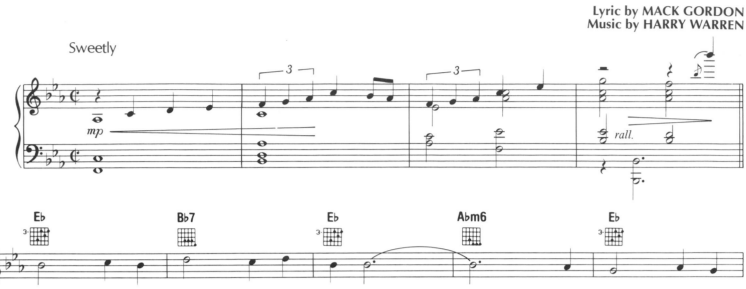

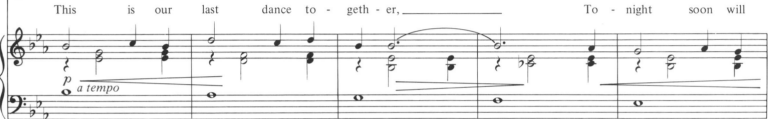

This is our last dance to-geth-er,_____ To-night soon will

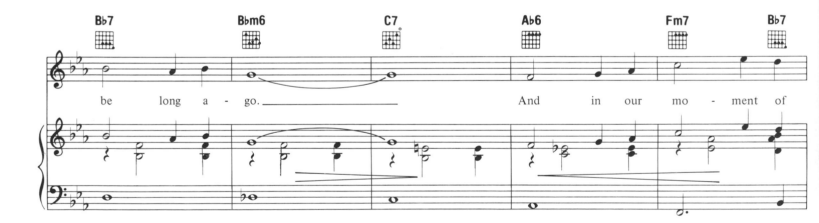

be long a-go._____ And in our mo-ment of

part-ing,_____ This is all I want you to know,_____

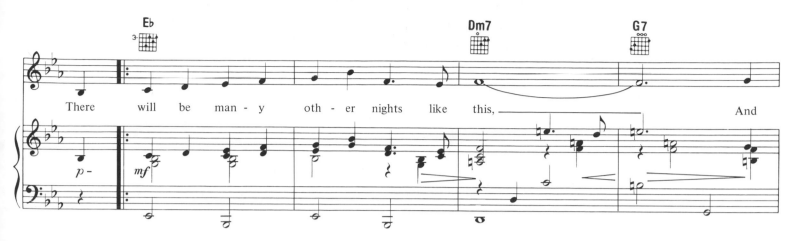

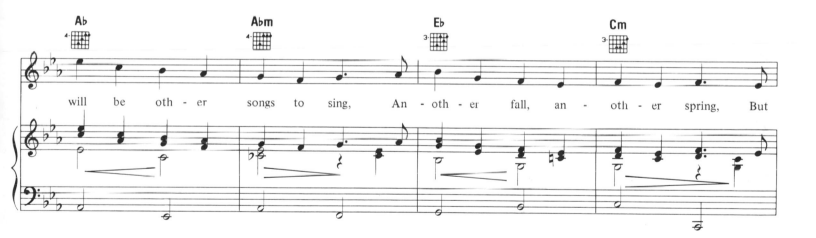

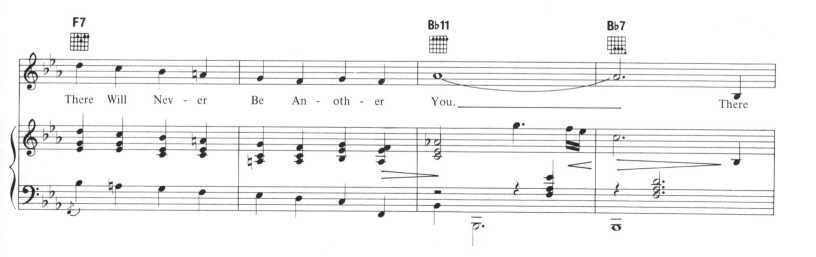

will be oth - er lips that I may kiss, _____ But

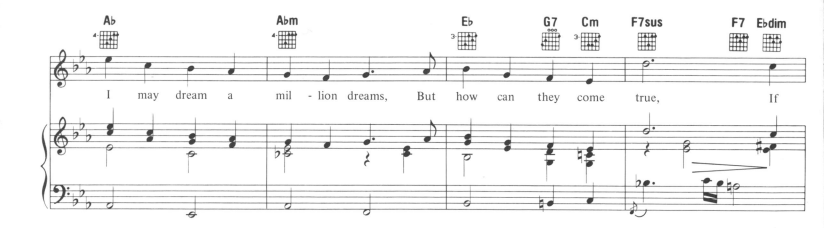

they won't thrill me like yours used to do, _____ Yes,

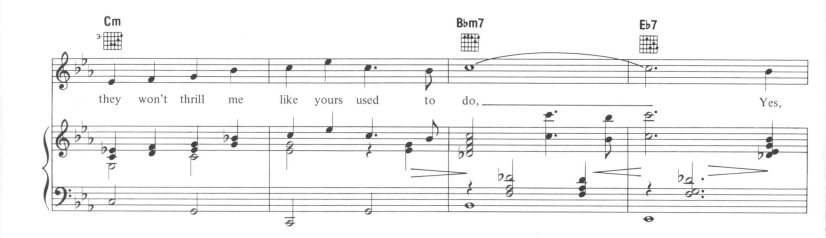

I may dream a mil - lion dreams, But how can they come true, If

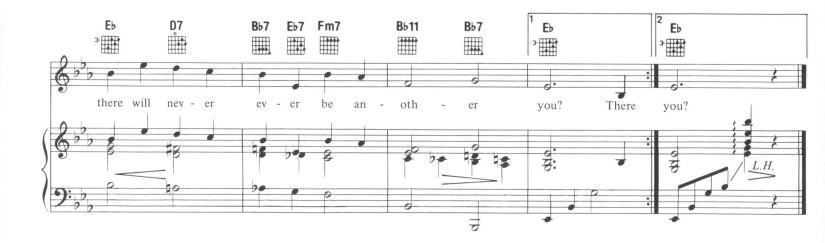

there will nev - er ev - er be an - oth - er you? There you?

THEY'RE PLAYING MY SONG

(From "THEY'RE PLAYING OUR SONG")

Word by CAROLE BAYER SAGER
Music by MARVIN HAMLISCH

Ho, ho, they're play-ing my song;_____ oh, yeah, they're play-ing my song_____ and when they're play-ing my song ev-'ry-bod-y's got-ta sh, sh, sh. Don't say a word__ now, lis-ten to that sweet mel-o-dy._____ I'm hap-py to say,__ in my

WE'RE IN THIS LOVE TOGETHER

Words and Music by
ROGER MURRAH
and KEITH STEGALL

189

I WENT TO A MARVELOUS PARTY

Words and Music by
NOEL COWARD

No - bod - y cares what peo - ple say, Tho' the Riv - ier - a Seems

real - ly much queer-er than Rome at its height. Yes - ter-day night I've been to a mar-vel-ous

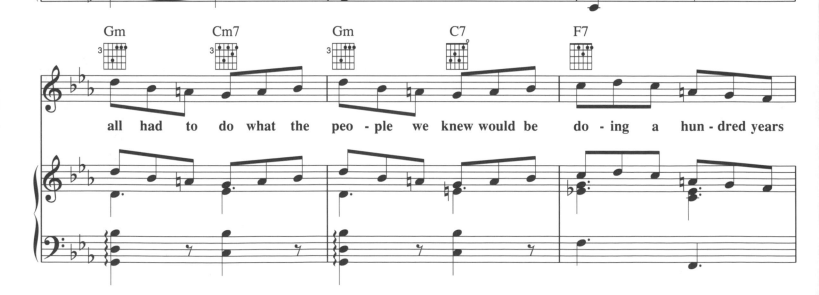

par - ty _____ I must say the fun was in - tense, _____ We

all had to do what the peo - ple we knew would be do - ing a hun - dred years

195

I'LL BE SEEING YOU

Lyrics by IRVING KAHAL
Music by SAMMY FAIN

197

NOTHING CAN STOP ME NOW!

(From the Musical Production
"THE ROAR OF THE GREASEPAINT – THE SMELL OF THE CROWD")

By LESLIE BRICUSSE
and ANTHONY NEWLY

Very Bright

Stand   well   back,   I'm
I   shall   find   suc-

com - ing   through___   Noth-ing   Can   Stop   Me   Now.___
cess to - day___   Noth-ing   Can   Stop   Me   Now.___

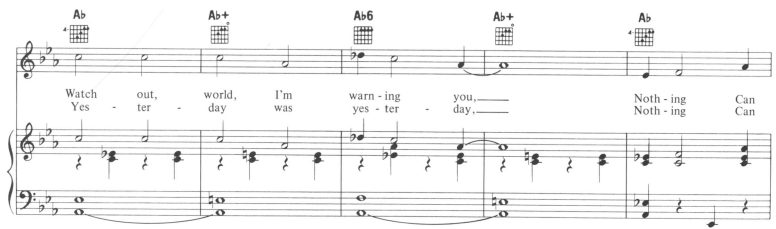

Watch   out,   world,   I'm   warn - ing   you,___   Noth - ing   Can
Yes - ter - day   I was   yes - ter - day,___   Noth - ing   Can

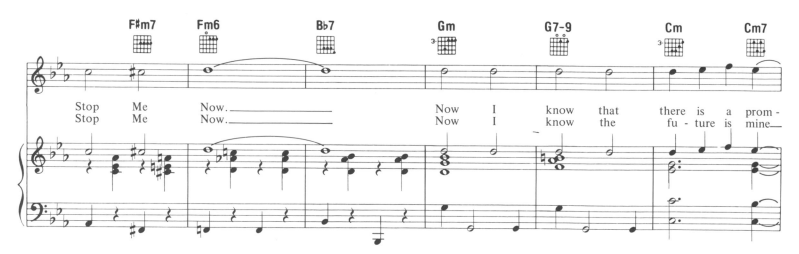

Stop   Me   Now.___   Now   I   know   that   there is   a   prom - ine
Stop   Me   Now.___   Now   I   know   the   fu - ture is   mine___

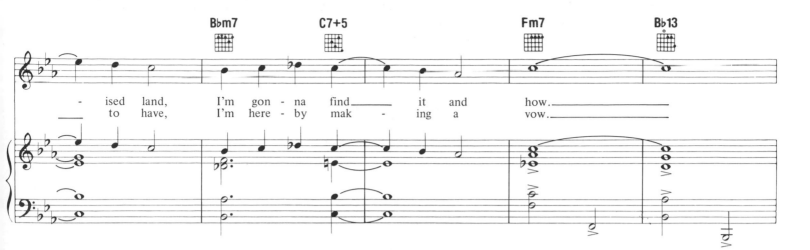

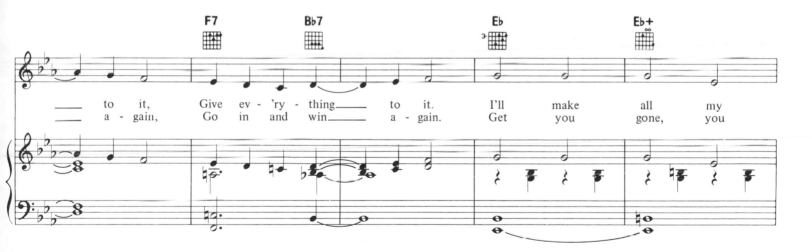

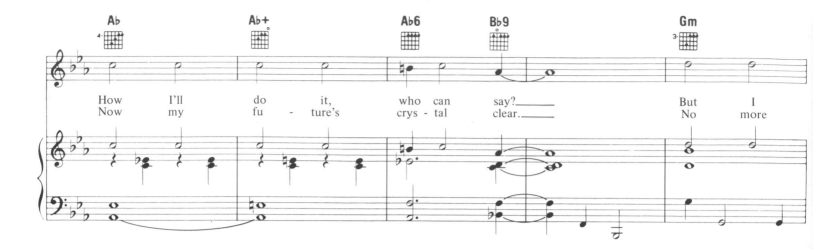

How I'll do it, who can say?_____ But I
Now my fu-ture's crys-tal clear._____ No more

know I will some day._____ I'm gon-na Watch out, world, I'm
woe for me to fear._____ I'm gon-na stand this world up-

on my way,_____ Noth-ing Can Stop____ Me Now.
on its ear,_____ And I'll suc-ceed____ Me some

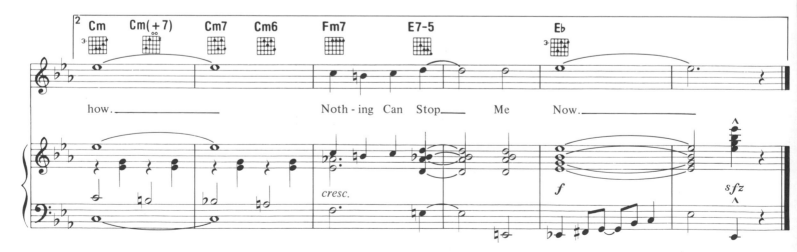

how._____ Noth-ing Can Stop____ Me Now._____

ONE
(From "A CHORUS LINE")

Music by MARVIN HAMLISCH
Lyric by EDWARD KLEBAN

206

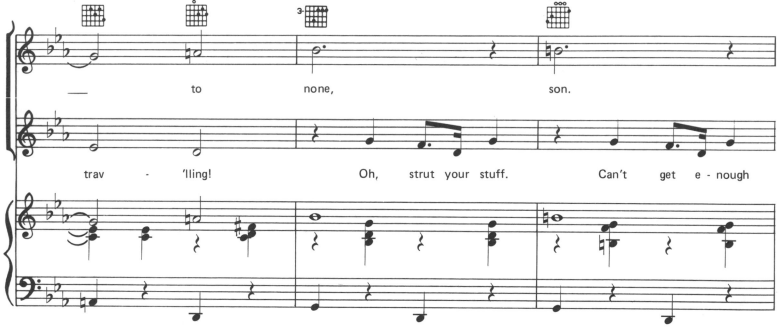

real - ly have to men - tion, she's the

her.

I'm a son of a gun, she is one of a

one?

kind.

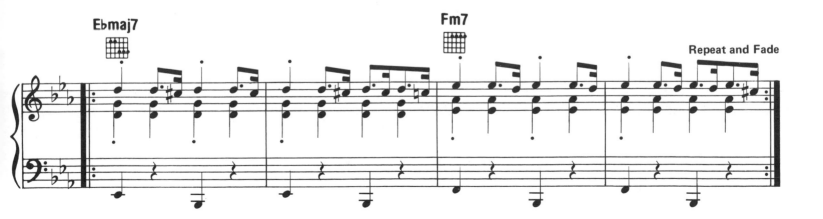

Repeat and Fade

PEOPLE
(From "FUNNY GIRL")

Words by BOB MERRILL
Music by JULE STYNE

THIS ONE'S FOR YOU

Words by MARTY PANZER
Music by BARRY MANILOW

221

THE LADY IS A TRAMP

(From "BABES IN ARMS")

Words by LORENZ HART
Music by RICHARD RODGERS

Moderato

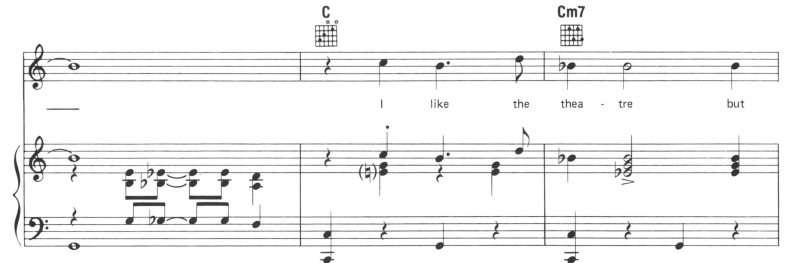

I get too hun-gry for din-ner at eight,___ I like the thea-tre but

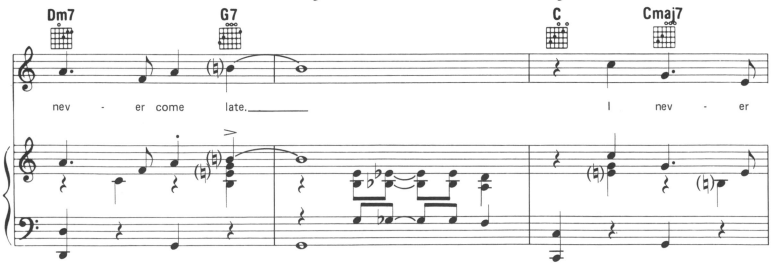

nev - er come late.___ I nev - er

Hate Cal - i - for - nia, It's cold and it's damp,____

That's why the la - dy is a tramp.____

la - dy is a tramp.____

MY WAY

Words by PAUL ANKA
Original French Lyric by GILLES THIBAULT
Music by CLAUDE FRANCOIS and JACQUES REVAUX

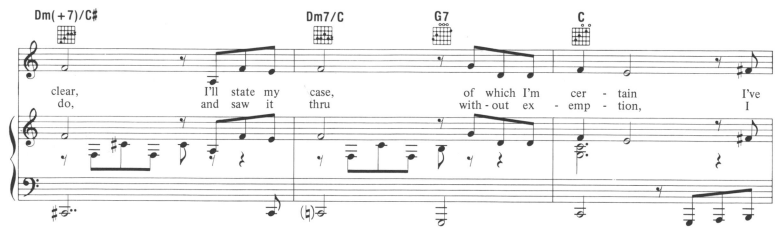

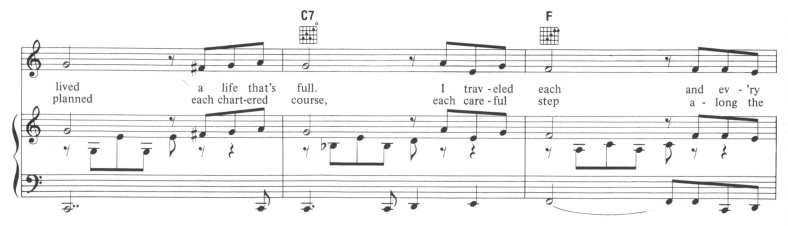

high-way, And more, much more than this, I did it My
by-way, And more, much more than this, I did it My

Way. Re - My
Way. Yes, there were times, I'm sure you

knew, when I bit off more than I could chew, But thru it all, when there was

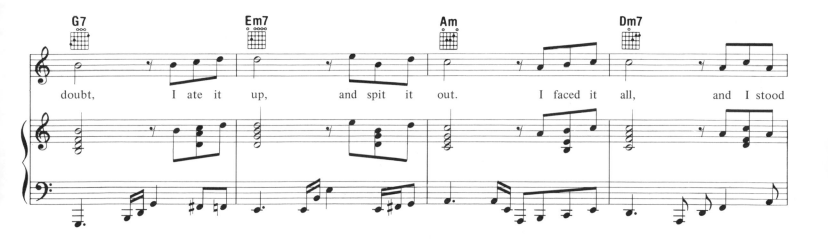

doubt, I ate it up, and spit it out. I faced it all, and I stood

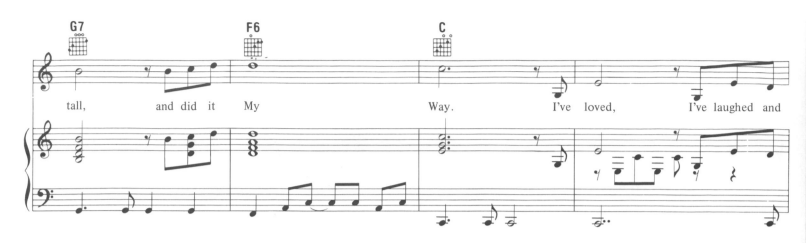

tall, and did it My Way. I've loved, I've laughed and

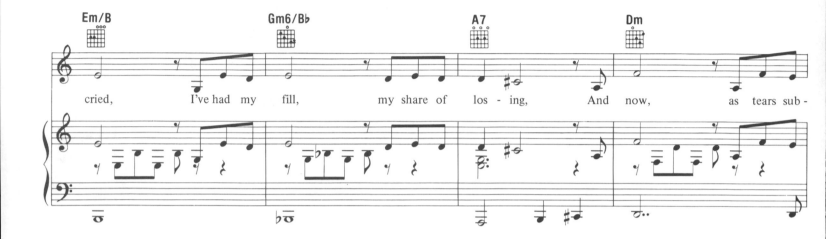

cried, I've had my fill, my share of los - ing, And now, as tears sub -

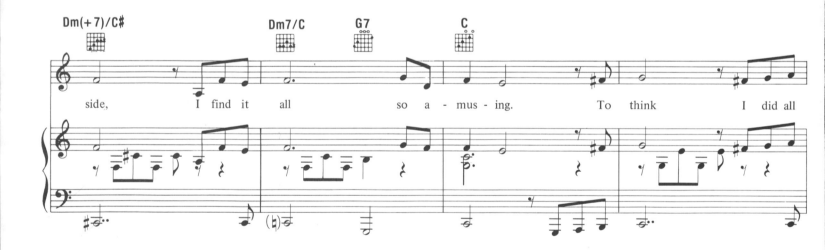

side, I find it all so a - mus - ing. To think I did all

that, and may I say, "Not in a shy way." Oh, no oh no, not

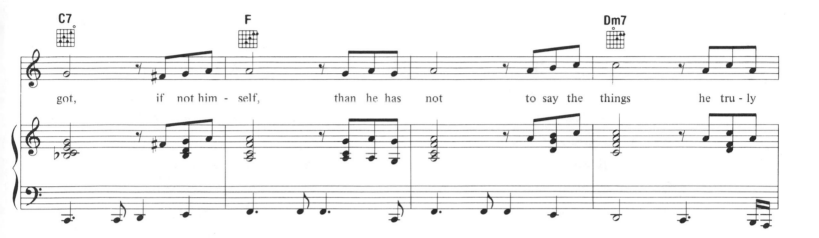

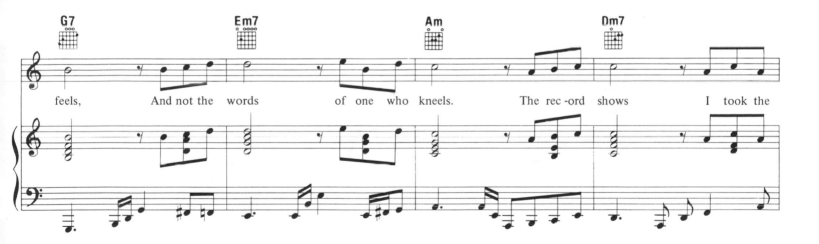

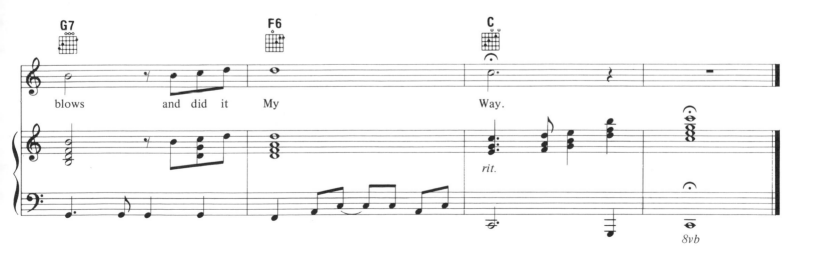

ALPHABETICAL INDEX
THE CABARET SONGBOOK

Classic Collections

FOR SINGERS

The Singer's Musical Theatre Anthology

The most comprehensive collection of Broadway selections ever organized specifically for the singer. Each of the five volumes contains important songs chosen because of their appropriateness to that particular voice type. All selections are in their authentic form, excerpted from the original vocal scores. The songs in THE SINGER'S MUSICAL THEATRE ANTHOLOGY, written by such noted composers as Kurt Weill, Richard Rodgers, Stephen Sondheim, and Jerome Kern, are vocal masterpieces ideal for the auditioning, practicing or performing vocalist.

Soprano
46 songs including: Where Or When • If I Loved You • Goodnight, My Someone • Smoke Gets In Your Eyes • Barbara Song • and many more.
00361071.......................................$17.95

Mezzo-Soprano or Alto
40 songs including: My Funny Valentine • I Love Paris • Don't Cry For Me Argentina • Losing My Mind • Send In The Clowns • and many more
00361072.......................................$17.95

Tenor
42 songs including: Stranger In Paradise • On The Street Where You Live • Younger Than Springtime • Lonely House • Not While I'm Around • and more.
00361073.......................................$17.95

Baritone or Bass
37 songs including: If Ever I Would Leave You • September Song • The Impossible Dream • Ol' Man River • Some Enchanted Evening • and more.
00361074.......................................$17.95

Duets
21 songs including: Too Many Mornings • We Kiss In A Shadow • People Will Say We're In Love • Bess You Is My Woman • Make Believe • more.
00361075.......................................$14.95

Musical Theater Classics

An exciting new series featuring the best songs from Broadway classics. Collections are organized by voice type and each book includes recorded piano accompaniment on cassette – ideal for practicing. Compiled by Richard Walters, Sue Malmberg, pianist.

Soprano, Volume 1
13 songs including: Climb Ev'ry Mountain • Falling In Love With Love • Hello, Young Lovers • Smoke Gets In Your Eyes • Wishing You Were Somehow Here Again.
00660148.......................................$14.95

Soprano, Volume 2
13 more favorites, including: Can't Help Lovin' Dat Man • I Could Have Danced All Night • Show Me • Think Of Me • Till There Was You.
00660149.......................................$14.95

Mezzo-Soprano/Alto, Volume 1
12 songs including: Don't Cry For Me Argentina • I Dreamed A Dream • The Lady Is A Tramp • People • and more.
00660150.......................................$14.95

Mezzo-Soprano/Alto, Volume 2
12 songs, including: Glad To Be Unhappy • Just You Wait • Memory • My Funny Valentine • On My Own • and more.
00660151.......................................$14.95

Tenor
12 songs including: All I Need Is A Girl • If You Could See Her • The Music Of The Night • On The Street Where You Live • Younger Than Springtime • and more.
00660152.......................................$14.95

Baritone/Bass
10 classics including: If Ever I Would Leave You • If I Loved You • Oh, What A Beautiful Mornin' • Ol' Man River • Try To Remember • and more.
00660153.......................................$14.95

Torch Songs

Sing your heart out with this collection of 60 famous melancholy favorites, including: Baby, Won't You Please Come Home • Bewitched • Can't Help Lovin' Dat Man • Cry Me A River • Here's That Rainy Day • Lush Life • The Man That Got Away • Misty • My Funny Valentine • The Party's Over • The Thrill Is Gone • Why Was I Born? • Woman Alone With The Blues • and more.
00490446.......................................$14.95

Cabaret Songs, Volumes 1 & 2

By William Bolcom
This is a collection of 12 songs primarily for the classical singer to perform in recital with piano accompaniment. The songs are in a medium voice range, and could probably be performed by any voice type (soprano, mezzo-soprano, etc.), although mezzo-sopranos will find them most suitable. The music has quite a theatrical flair, although it is in a contemporary classical style.
00008273.......................................$14.95

The Entertainers' Songbook

A singer's handbook for auditions and club acts. Over 70 titles, including some of the best songs for auditions: Standards and showtunes, popular and rock, blues-folk-jazz, and country and western.
00312120.......................................$14.95

Prices, availability and contents subject to change without notice.
Prices may vary outside the U.S.A.
Certain products may not be available in all territories outside the U.S.A.

For more information, see your local music dealer, or write to:
Hal Leonard Publishing Corporation
P.O. Box 13819 Milwaukee, Wisconsin 53213